# 50 Holiday Feast Recipes for Home

By: Kelly Johnson

# Table of Contents

- Classic Scones with Clotted Cream and Jam
- Lemon Drizzle Cake
- Victoria Sponge Cake
- Cucumber Tea Sandwiches
- Earl Grey Shortbread Cookies
- Chocolate Eclairs
- Mini Quiches
- Raspberry Almond Bars
- Blueberry Muffins
- Mini Chicken and Leek Pies
- Lemon Madeleines
- Cheese Scones
- Chocolate Brownies
- Orange Cranberry Loaf
- Pistachio Macarons
- Tea-Infused Truffles
- Smoked Salmon Pinwheels
- Lavender Honey Cake
- Cheddar and Chive Biscuits
- Strawberry Cream Puffs
- Lemon Tartlets
- Mini Pavlovas with Berries
- Spinach and Feta Triangles
- Chocolate Chip Cookies
- Carrot Cake Cupcakes
- Elderflower Cupcakes
- Almond Crescents
- Tea-Infused Panna Cotta
- Apricot Rugelach
- Mini Tarts with Fruit Compote
- Cheese Straws
- Walnut and Date Bars
- Lemon Poppy Seed Muffins
- Cherry Bakewell Tartlets
- Matcha Swirl Pound Cake

- Coconut Macaroons
- Mini Pizzas
- Rosewater Shortbread
- Mini Eclairs with Coffee Cream
- Gingerbread Cookies
- Fig and Goat Cheese Crostini
- Linzer Cookies
- Sausage Rolls
- Apple Turnovers
- Chocolate Hazelnut Biscotti
- Plum Cake
- Mini Lemon Tarts
- Nutella Swirl Brownies
- Raspberry Ripple Cheesecake Bars
- Green Tea Ice Cream

**Classic Scones with Clotted Cream and Jam**

Ingredients:

- 2 cups all-purpose flour
- 1/4 cup granulated sugar
- 1 tablespoon baking powder
- 1/2 teaspoon salt
- 1/3 cup unsalted butter, cold and cubed
- 2/3 cup milk (plus extra for brushing)
- 1 teaspoon vanilla extract
- Clotted cream, for serving
- Strawberry jam or raspberry jam, for serving

Instructions:

Preheat the Oven:
- Preheat your oven to 400°F (200°C). Line a baking sheet with parchment paper.

Mix Dry Ingredients:
- In a large bowl, whisk together the flour, sugar, baking powder, and salt.

Cut in Butter:
- Add the cold cubed butter to the flour mixture.
- Use a pastry cutter or your fingers to rub the butter into the flour until the mixture resembles coarse crumbs.

Combine Wet Ingredients:
- In a separate bowl, whisk together the milk and vanilla extract.

Form Dough:
- Make a well in the center of the flour mixture.
- Pour the milk mixture into the well.
- Gently stir until the dough comes together. Be careful not to overmix.

Shape and Cut Scones:
- Transfer the dough onto a lightly floured surface.
- Pat the dough into a circle about 3/4-inch thick.
- Use a round biscuit cutter (about 2 inches in diameter) to cut out scones. Gather and re-roll the dough scraps as needed.

Bake the Scones:
- Place the scones on the prepared baking sheet.
- Brush the tops of the scones with a little milk.
- Bake for 12-15 minutes, or until the scones are golden brown and cooked through.

Serve:
- Allow the scones to cool slightly on a wire rack.
- Serve warm with clotted cream and strawberry or raspberry jam.

Notes:

- For best results, handle the dough gently and avoid overworking it to keep the scones light and fluffy.
- You can customize these scones by adding raisins or currants to the dough before shaping.
- Enjoy these classic scones as a delightful treat for afternoon tea or brunch, paired with clotted cream and your favorite jam.

**Lemon Drizzle Cake**

Ingredients:

- 1 1/2 cups all-purpose flour
- 1 teaspoon baking powder
- 1/4 teaspoon salt
- 1 cup granulated sugar
- 3 large eggs
- 1/2 cup unsalted butter, melted
- Zest of 2 lemons
- Juice of 1 1/2 lemons (about 4-5 tablespoons)
- 1/2 cup powdered sugar (for the drizzle)

Instructions:

Preheat the Oven:
- Preheat your oven to 350°F (175°C). Grease and line a 9x5-inch loaf pan with parchment paper.

Mix Dry Ingredients:
- In a bowl, whisk together the flour, baking powder, and salt. Set aside.

Combine Wet Ingredients:
- In a separate large bowl, whisk together the granulated sugar and eggs until pale and creamy.
- Gradually whisk in the melted butter.

Add Lemon Zest and Juice:
- Stir in the lemon zest and lemon juice into the wet mixture.

Incorporate Dry Ingredients:
- Gradually fold the dry flour mixture into the wet ingredients until just combined. Be careful not to overmix.

Bake the Cake:
- Pour the batter into the prepared loaf pan and spread it evenly.

Bake for 45-50 minutes, or until a toothpick inserted into the center comes out clean.

Prepare the Drizzle:
- While the cake is baking, mix the powdered sugar with the remaining lemon juice (about 1 tablespoon) to make the drizzle.

Drizzle the Cake:
- Once the cake is out of the oven and still warm, poke holes all over the surface with a skewer or fork.
- Pour the lemon drizzle evenly over the warm cake, allowing it to soak in.

Cool and Serve:
- Let the cake cool in the pan for 10 minutes, then transfer it to a wire rack to cool completely.

- Slice and serve the lemon drizzle cake. Enjoy!

Notes:

- You can adjust the amount of lemon juice in the drizzle to achieve your desired level of tartness.
- This cake is best enjoyed on the day it's made but can be stored in an airtight container for a few days.
- Serve slices of lemon drizzle cake with a cup of tea or coffee for a delightful afternoon treat. The tangy lemon flavor and moist texture make it a favorite for tea time or any time of day!

**Cucumber Tea Sandwiches**

Ingredients:

- 1 English cucumber, thinly sliced
- 8 slices of white or whole wheat sandwich bread (remove crusts if desired)
- 4 ounces cream cheese, softened
- 1-2 tablespoons mayonnaise
- Fresh dill, chopped
- Salt and pepper, to taste

Instructions:

Prepare the Cucumbers:
- Wash the cucumber and thinly slice it using a mandoline or sharp knife. Pat the slices dry with paper towels to remove excess moisture.

Mix Cream Cheese Spread:
- In a bowl, combine the softened cream cheese and mayonnaise. Start with 1 tablespoon of mayonnaise and add more if needed to achieve a smooth and spreadable consistency.

Season the Spread:
- Add chopped fresh dill, salt, and pepper to taste to the cream cheese mixture. Mix well to incorporate the flavors.

Assemble the Sandwiches:
- Lay out the bread slices on a clean work surface.
- Spread a generous layer of the cream cheese mixture onto each slice of bread, covering evenly.

Add Cucumber Slices:
- Arrange the thinly sliced cucumber on half of the bread slices, covering the cream cheese layer.

Top and Slice:
- Place the remaining bread slices on top of the cucumber to form sandwiches.
- Use a sharp knife to cut each sandwich into desired shapes, such as triangles or rectangles.

Serve:
- Arrange the cucumber tea sandwiches on a serving platter.
- Garnish with additional fresh dill, if desired.
- Serve immediately as part of a traditional afternoon tea or a light lunch.

Notes:

- For a refreshing twist, you can sprinkle a little lemon zest or finely chopped mint into the cream cheese mixture.
- These sandwiches can be made ahead of time and stored in the refrigerator covered with a damp paper towel to prevent the bread from drying out.
- Cucumber tea sandwiches are a classic and elegant addition to any tea party or gathering. Enjoy their light and refreshing flavors paired with a cup of your favorite tea!

**Earl Grey Shortbread Cookies**

Ingredients:

- 1 cup unsalted butter, softened
- 1/2 cup granulated sugar
- 2 cups all-purpose flour
- 2 tablespoons finely ground Earl Grey tea leaves (from about 4-5 tea bags)
- 1/4 teaspoon salt
- Optional: Extra granulated sugar for sprinkling

Instructions:

Prepare the Earl Grey Tea:
- Using a mortar and pestle or a spice grinder, finely grind the contents of 4-5 Earl Grey tea bags until you have 2 tablespoons of finely ground tea leaves. Set aside.

Cream Butter and Sugar:
- In a large bowl, cream together the softened butter and granulated sugar until light and fluffy.

Add Dry Ingredients:
- Add the flour, finely ground Earl Grey tea leaves, and salt to the butter-sugar mixture.

Mix Until Combined:
- Mix the ingredients together until a dough forms. Be careful not to overmix.

Shape the Dough:
- Transfer the dough onto a lightly floured surface.
- Shape the dough into a log about 2 inches in diameter.

Chill the Dough:
- Wrap the dough in plastic wrap and refrigerate for at least 1 hour, or until firm.

Preheat the Oven:
- Preheat your oven to 350°F (175°C). Line a baking sheet with parchment paper.

Slice the Cookies:
- Remove the chilled dough from the refrigerator.
- Slice the dough into rounds about 1/4 inch thick.

Place on Baking Sheet:
- Arrange the cookies on the prepared baking sheet, spacing them slightly apart.

Optional: Sprinkle with Sugar:
- If desired, sprinkle the tops of the cookies with a little extra granulated sugar for added sweetness and texture.

Bake the Cookies:
- Bake in the preheated oven for 12-15 minutes, or until the edges are lightly golden.

Cool and Enjoy:
- Allow the cookies to cool on the baking sheet for a few minutes before transferring them to a wire rack to cool completely.

Notes:

- Make sure to use unsalted butter for this recipe to control the saltiness.
- Adjust the amount of Earl Grey tea leaves based on your preference for tea flavor intensity.
- These Earl Grey shortbread cookies are perfect for enjoying with a cup of tea or as a delightful treat for tea time. The subtle floral notes of Earl Grey tea add a unique and delicious twist to classic shortbread cookies. Enjoy!

**Chocolate Eclairs**

Ingredients:

*For the Choux Pastry:*

- 1/2 cup water
- 1/2 cup whole milk
- 1/2 cup unsalted butter
- 1 tablespoon granulated sugar
- 1/4 teaspoon salt
- 1 cup all-purpose flour
- 4 large eggs

*For the Filling:*

- 1 1/2 cups heavy cream
- 1 teaspoon vanilla extract
- 3 tablespoons powdered sugar

*For the Chocolate Glaze:*

- 1/2 cup dark or semi-sweet chocolate chips
- 2 tablespoons unsalted butter
- 1 tablespoon corn syrup (optional, for shine)

Instructions:

Prepare the Choux Pastry:
- In a medium saucepan, combine water, milk, butter, sugar, and salt. Bring to a boil over medium heat.
- Reduce heat to low, add flour all at once, and stir vigorously until the mixture forms a smooth dough that pulls away from the sides of the pan.
- Transfer the dough to a mixing bowl and let it cool slightly for about 5 minutes.
- Add eggs, one at a time, beating well after each addition, until the dough is smooth and glossy.

Pipe and Bake the Eclairs:
- Preheat the oven to 400°F (200°C) and line a baking sheet with parchment paper.
- Transfer the choux pastry dough into a piping bag fitted with a large round tip.

- Pipe 4-inch long strips of dough onto the prepared baking sheet, leaving space between each eclair.
- Bake for 15 minutes at 400°F (200°C), then reduce the oven temperature to 350°F (180°C) and bake for an additional 20-25 minutes, or until the eclairs are golden brown and puffed.

Prepare the Filling:
- In a mixing bowl, whip the heavy cream, vanilla extract, and powdered sugar until stiff peaks form.
- Transfer the whipped cream into a piping bag fitted with a small round tip.

Fill the Eclairs:
- Once the eclairs are completely cool, use a small knife to make a small slit on one side of each eclair.
- Pipe the whipped cream filling into each eclair through the slit until they are filled.

Make the Chocolate Glaze:
- In a microwave-safe bowl, combine the chocolate chips, butter, and corn syrup (if using).
- Microwave in 30-second intervals, stirring between each interval, until the chocolate is melted and smooth.

Glaze the Eclairs:
- Dip the top of each eclair into the melted chocolate glaze, allowing any excess to drip off.

Chill and Serve:
- Place the glazed eclairs on a wire rack to set the chocolate glaze.
- Chill the eclairs in the refrigerator for about 30 minutes to allow the filling to set.
- Serve chilled and enjoy these delicious homemade chocolate eclairs!

Notes:

- Be sure to fill the eclairs just before serving to keep them fresh and avoid soggy pastry.
- You can customize the filling by adding other flavors such as pastry cream or flavored whipped cream.
- These chocolate eclairs make an elegant and delightful treat for any occasion, especially for tea time or dessert. Enjoy the light and airy choux pastry filled with creamy whipped cream and topped with rich chocolate glaze!

Mini Quiches

Ingredients:

- 1 package (14 ounces) frozen puff pastry, thawed
- 6 large eggs
- 1/2 cup heavy cream
- Salt and pepper, to taste

- 1 cup shredded cheese (such as cheddar, Swiss, or Gruyere)
- 1/2 cup diced cooked ham or bacon bits
- 1/4 cup chopped green onions or chives
- Optional: Other fillings such as spinach, mushrooms, or bell peppers

Instructions:

Preheat the Oven:
- Preheat your oven to 375°F (190°C). Lightly grease a mini muffin tin or tartlet pans.

Prepare the Puff Pastry:
- On a lightly floured surface, roll out the thawed puff pastry dough to about 1/8-inch thickness.
- Use a round cookie cutter or a glass to cut out circles slightly larger than the size of the mini muffin tin cups.

Line the Muffin Tin:
- Gently press the pastry circles into each mini muffin cup, forming small tart shells. Trim any excess dough if necessary.

Prepare the Quiche Filling:
- In a mixing bowl, whisk together the eggs, heavy cream, salt, and pepper until well combined.
- Stir in the shredded cheese, diced ham or bacon bits, chopped green onions or chives, and any other desired fillings.

Fill the Tart Shells:
- Spoon the quiche filling mixture evenly into each pastry-lined mini muffin cup, filling almost to the top.

Bake the Mini Quiches:
- Place the mini muffin tin in the preheated oven.
- Bake for 15-20 minutes, or until the quiches are puffed and golden brown on top.

Cool and Serve:
- Allow the mini quiches to cool in the pan for a few minutes before carefully removing them.
- Serve warm or at room temperature as delightful appetizers or snacks.

Notes:

- Feel free to customize the fillings based on your preferences. You can add cooked spinach, sautéed mushrooms, diced bell peppers, or other ingredients you enjoy in quiche.
- These mini quiches are great for parties, brunches, or as a part of a tea time spread.
- Store any leftover mini quiches in an airtight container in the refrigerator and reheat gently in the oven before serving. Enjoy these delicious bite-sized treats!

**Raspberry Almond Bars**

Ingredients:

*For the Crust:*

- 1 cup all-purpose flour
- 1/2 cup unsalted butter, softened
- 1/4 cup granulated sugar
- 1/4 teaspoon almond extract

*For the Filling:*

- 1/2 cup raspberry jam or preserves
- 1/2 cup fresh raspberries (optional)

*For the Almond Topping:*

- 1/2 cup unsalted butter, melted
- 1/2 cup granulated sugar
- 1 teaspoon almond extract
- 1 cup almond flour (or finely ground almonds)
- 1/4 cup sliced almonds

Instructions:

Preheat the Oven:
- Preheat your oven to 350°F (175°C). Grease or line an 8-inch square baking pan with parchment paper.

Make the Crust:
- In a mixing bowl, combine the flour, softened butter, sugar, and almond extract.
- Mix until crumbly and well combined.

Press Into Pan:
- Press the crust mixture evenly into the bottom of the prepared baking pan.

Add Raspberry Filling:
- Spread the raspberry jam or preserves over the crust layer.
- If using fresh raspberries, scatter them over the raspberry jam layer.

Prepare the Almond Topping:
- In another bowl, whisk together the melted butter, sugar, and almond extract until well combined.
- Stir in the almond flour (or finely ground almonds) until a thick batter forms.

Spread Over Raspberry Layer:
- Spread the almond topping mixture evenly over the raspberry filling.

Add Sliced Almonds:
- Sprinkle the sliced almonds over the top of the almond batter.

Bake the Bars:
- Bake in the preheated oven for 25-30 minutes, or until the top is golden brown and the edges are slightly bubbly.

Cool and Slice:
- Allow the raspberry almond bars to cool completely in the pan on a wire rack.
- Once cooled, lift the bars out of the pan using the parchment paper edges.
- Cut into squares or bars using a sharp knife.

Serve and Enjoy:
- Serve these delicious raspberry almond bars as a sweet treat for dessert, tea time, or any occasion!

Notes:

- You can customize these bars by using different types of jam or preserves, such as strawberry or apricot.
- Store any leftover bars in an airtight container at room temperature for a few days or in the refrigerator for longer freshness.
- These bars can be made ahead of time and are perfect for sharing with friends and family. Enjoy the delightful combination of raspberry and almond flavors in every bite!

**Blueberry Muffins**

Ingredients:

- 2 cups all-purpose flour
- 1/2 cup granulated sugar
- 1 tablespoon baking powder
- 1/2 teaspoon salt
- 1/2 cup unsalted butter, melted and cooled slightly
- 2 large eggs
- 1 cup milk
- 1 teaspoon vanilla extract
- 1 1/2 cups fresh or frozen blueberries (if using frozen, do not thaw)

Instructions:

Preheat the Oven:
- Preheat your oven to 375°F (190°C). Line a muffin tin with paper liners or grease with cooking spray.

Mix Dry Ingredients:
- In a large bowl, whisk together the flour, sugar, baking powder, and salt.

Combine Wet Ingredients:
- In another bowl, whisk together the melted butter, eggs, milk, and vanilla extract until well combined.

Combine Wet and Dry Ingredients:
- Pour the wet ingredients into the bowl of dry ingredients.
- Stir gently with a spatula until just combined. Be careful not to overmix; it's okay if the batter is a bit lumpy.

Fold in Blueberries:
- Gently fold in the blueberries until evenly distributed throughout the batter.

Fill Muffin Cups:
- Divide the batter evenly among the prepared muffin cups, filling each cup about 2/3 to 3/4 full.

Bake the Muffins:
- Bake in the preheated oven for 18-20 minutes, or until the tops are golden brown and a toothpick inserted into the center of a muffin comes out clean.

Cool and Serve:
- Remove the muffins from the oven and let them cool in the pan for a few minutes.
- Transfer the muffins to a wire rack to cool completely before serving.

Notes:

- You can add a sprinkle of coarse sugar on top of the muffins before baking for a nice crunch.
- If using frozen blueberries, do not thaw them before adding to the batter to prevent excess moisture.
- Feel free to add lemon zest or a dash of cinnamon to the batter for extra flavor variations.
- These blueberry muffins are perfect for breakfast, brunch, or a delightful snack. Enjoy them warm or at room temperature with a cup of tea or coffee!

**Mini Chicken and Leek Pies**

Ingredients:

*For the Filling:*

- 2 tablespoons unsalted butter
- 1 leek, thinly sliced (white and light green parts only)
- 1 clove garlic, minced
- 1 pound boneless, skinless chicken breasts, diced
- Salt and pepper, to taste
- 1/4 cup all-purpose flour
- 1 cup chicken broth
- 1/2 cup heavy cream
- 1/2 cup frozen peas (optional)
- 1 tablespoon chopped fresh thyme (or 1 teaspoon dried thyme)

*For the Pie Crust:*

- 1 package (14 ounces) refrigerated pie crusts (or homemade pie dough)

Instructions:

Preheat the Oven:
- Preheat your oven to 375°F (190°C). Grease a muffin tin or use silicone muffin cups for mini pies.

Prepare the Filling:
- In a large skillet, melt the butter over medium heat.
- Add the sliced leeks and minced garlic, and sauté until softened, about 3-4 minutes.

Cook Chicken:
- Add the diced chicken to the skillet. Season with salt and pepper.
- Cook until the chicken is no longer pink, about 5-6 minutes.

Make the Sauce:
- Sprinkle the flour over the chicken and leek mixture. Stir well to coat evenly.
- Pour in the chicken broth and heavy cream, stirring constantly.
- Cook until the mixture thickens, about 3-4 minutes.
- Stir in the frozen peas (if using) and chopped thyme. Remove from heat and set aside.

Prepare the Pie Crust:
- Roll out the pie crusts on a lightly floured surface.

- Use a round cookie cutter or a glass to cut out circles slightly larger than the size of your muffin cups.

Assemble the Mini Pies:
- Gently press the pie crust circles into the greased muffin tin cups, lining the bottom and sides.

Fill the Pies:
- Spoon the chicken and leek filling evenly into each pie crust.

Add Top Crust:
- Use another piece of pie crust to cover each mini pie. You can leave them open-faced or use a smaller round cutter to create a decorative top crust.

Bake the Pies:
- Place the muffin tin in the preheated oven and bake for 20-25 minutes, or until the crusts are golden brown and the filling is bubbly.

Cool and Serve:
- Allow the mini chicken and leek pies to cool in the muffin tin for a few minutes before carefully removing them.
- Serve warm as appetizers, snacks, or part of a meal.

Notes:

- Feel free to add other vegetables like carrots or mushrooms to the filling for extra flavor and texture.
- These mini pies can be made ahead of time and stored in the refrigerator. Reheat in the oven before serving.
- Enjoy these delicious and savory mini chicken and leek pies for a delightful treat or party appetizer!

**Lemon Madeleines**

Ingredients:

- 2/3 cup all-purpose flour
- 1/2 teaspoon baking powder
- 1/4 teaspoon salt
- 1/2 cup granulated sugar
- Zest of 1 lemon
- 2 large eggs
- 1 teaspoon vanilla extract
- 1/4 cup unsalted butter, melted and cooled
- Powdered sugar, for dusting (optional)

Instructions:

Preheat the Oven:
- Preheat your oven to 375°F (190°C). Grease a madeleine pan or mini muffin tin with butter or non-stick cooking spray.

Prepare Dry Ingredients:
- In a small bowl, whisk together the flour, baking powder, and salt. Set aside.

Mix Sugar and Lemon Zest:
- In a mixing bowl, rub the lemon zest into the granulated sugar with your fingers until fragrant and well combined.

Add Eggs and Vanilla:
- Add the eggs to the sugar-zest mixture and beat with an electric mixer on medium-high speed until pale and fluffy, about 2-3 minutes.
- Beat in the vanilla extract.

Fold in Dry Ingredients:
- Gently fold the flour mixture into the egg-sugar mixture using a spatula until just combined.

Incorporate Melted Butter:
- Pour the melted and cooled butter into the batter and gently fold until incorporated.

Fill Madeleine Pan:
- Spoon the batter into the prepared madeleine pan, filling each shell about 3/4 full.

Bake the Madeleines:
- Bake in the preheated oven for 10-12 minutes, or until the madeleines are golden brown around the edges and spring back when lightly touched.

Cool and Dust with Powdered Sugar:
- Remove the madeleines from the oven and let them cool in the pan for a few minutes.
- Gently transfer the madeleines to a wire rack to cool completely.

- Dust with powdered sugar before serving, if desired.

Notes:

- Madeleines are best enjoyed fresh but can be stored in an airtight container at room temperature for up to 2 days.
- For variation, you can add a tablespoon of lemon juice to the batter for extra lemon flavor.
- Serve these delicate and citrusy lemon madeleines with tea or coffee for a delightful afternoon treat. Enjoy their light and airy texture and bright lemony flavor!

**Cheese Scones**

Ingredients:

- 2 cups all-purpose flour
- 1 tablespoon baking powder
- 1/2 teaspoon salt
- 1/4 cup unsalted butter, cold and cubed
- 1 cup grated sharp cheddar cheese
- 1/2 cup buttermilk (or milk with a splash of vinegar)
- 1 large egg, beaten (for egg wash)
- Optional: Additional grated cheese for topping

Instructions:

Preheat the Oven:
- Preheat your oven to 400°F (200°C). Line a baking sheet with parchment paper.

Mix Dry Ingredients:
- In a large bowl, whisk together the flour, baking powder, and salt.

Cut in Butter:
- Add the cold cubed butter to the flour mixture.
- Use a pastry cutter or your fingers to work the butter into the flour until the mixture resembles coarse crumbs.

Add Grated Cheese:
- Stir in the grated cheddar cheese until evenly distributed in the flour mixture.

Combine Wet Ingredients:
- In a small bowl, whisk together the buttermilk and beaten egg.

Form Dough:
- Make a well in the center of the flour mixture.
- Pour the buttermilk mixture into the well.
- Gently stir with a fork or spatula until the dough starts to come together.

Knead the Dough:
- Transfer the dough onto a lightly floured surface.
- Knead the dough gently a few times until it holds together. Be careful not to overwork the dough.

Shape and Cut Scones:
- Pat the dough into a circle about 1-inch thick.
- Use a round biscuit cutter (about 2 inches in diameter) to cut out scones. Press straight down without twisting the cutter to ensure even rising.

Brush with Egg Wash:
- Place the scones on the prepared baking sheet.
- Brush the tops of the scones with the remaining beaten egg.
- Optionally, sprinkle some additional grated cheese on top of each scone.

Bake the Scones:
- Bake in the preheated oven for 12-15 minutes, or until the scones are golden brown and cooked through.

Cool and Serve:
- Transfer the scones to a wire rack to cool slightly before serving.

Notes:

- Serve these warm cheese scones with butter or cream cheese for a delightful snack or breakfast.
- You can customize these scones by adding chopped herbs like chives or thyme for extra flavor.
- Store any leftover scones in an airtight container at room temperature for up to 2 days. Reheat briefly in the microwave or oven before serving. Enjoy!

**Chocolate Brownies**

Ingredients:

- 1 cup (2 sticks) unsalted butter, melted
- 2 cups granulated sugar
- 4 large eggs
- 2 teaspoons vanilla extract
- 1 cup all-purpose flour
- 3/4 cup unsweetened cocoa powder
- 1/2 teaspoon salt
- 1 cup chocolate chips or chopped chocolate (optional)

Instructions:

Preheat the Oven:
- Preheat your oven to 350°F (175°C). Grease a 9x13-inch baking pan or line it with parchment paper.

Mix Wet Ingredients:
- In a large bowl, whisk together the melted butter and granulated sugar until well combined.

Add Eggs and Vanilla:
- Whisk in the eggs, one at a time, until fully incorporated.
- Stir in the vanilla extract.

Combine Dry Ingredients:
- In a separate bowl, sift together the flour, cocoa powder, and salt.

Combine Wet and Dry Mixtures:
- Gradually add the dry ingredients to the wet ingredients, mixing until just combined. Be careful not to overmix.

Add Chocolate Chips (Optional):
- Fold in the chocolate chips or chopped chocolate into the batter, if using.

Pour Batter into Pan:
- Pour the brownie batter into the prepared baking pan, spreading it out evenly with a spatula.

Bake the Brownies:
- Bake in the preheated oven for 25-30 minutes, or until a toothpick inserted into the center comes out with a few moist crumbs attached.

Cool and Serve:
- Allow the brownies to cool completely in the pan on a wire rack.
- Once cooled, cut into squares and serve.

Notes:

- For fudgier brownies, bake them on the shorter end of the baking time. For cake-like brownies, bake them closer to the longer end of the baking time.
- You can add chopped nuts such as walnuts or pecans to the brownie batter for extra texture.
- Store leftover brownies in an airtight container at room temperature for a few days, or in the refrigerator for longer storage. Enjoy these classic chocolate brownies as a delightful treat!

**Orange Cranberry Loaf**

Ingredients:

- 1/2 cup unsalted butter, softened
- 1 cup granulated sugar
- 2 large eggs
- 1 teaspoon vanilla extract
- Zest of 1 orange
- 1/2 cup fresh orange juice
- 1 3/4 cups all-purpose flour
- 1 teaspoon baking powder
- 1/4 teaspoon baking soda
- 1/4 teaspoon salt
- 1 cup fresh or frozen cranberries (if using frozen, do not thaw)
- Optional: 1/2 cup chopped nuts (such as pecans or walnuts)

For the Orange Glaze (Optional):

- 1 cup powdered sugar
- 2-3 tablespoons fresh orange juice

Instructions:

Preheat the Oven:
- Preheat your oven to 350°F (175°C). Grease a 9x5-inch loaf pan and line it with parchment paper for easy removal.

Cream Butter and Sugar:
- In a large mixing bowl, cream together the softened butter and granulated sugar until light and fluffy.

Add Eggs and Flavorings:
- Beat in the eggs, one at a time, until well combined.
- Mix in the vanilla extract and orange zest.

Combine Dry Ingredients:
- In a separate bowl, whisk together the flour, baking powder, baking soda, and salt.

Alternate Mixing:
- Gradually add the dry ingredients to the wet ingredients, alternating with the fresh orange juice, beginning and ending with the dry ingredients. Mix until just combined.

Fold in Cranberries and Nuts:
- Gently fold in the cranberries and chopped nuts (if using) into the batter.

**Bake the Loaf:**
- Pour the batter into the prepared loaf pan, spreading it out evenly.

**Bake Until Golden:**
- Bake in the preheated oven for 50-60 minutes, or until a toothpick inserted into the center comes out clean.

**Cool in Pan:**
- Allow the loaf to cool in the pan for about 10 minutes, then transfer it to a wire rack to cool completely.

**Prepare the Orange Glaze (Optional):**
- In a small bowl, whisk together the powdered sugar and fresh orange juice until smooth and drizzling consistency.

**Glaze the Loaf:**
- Drizzle the orange glaze over the cooled loaf.

**Slice and Serve:**
- Once the glaze has set, slice the orange cranberry loaf and serve.

**Notes:**

- This orange cranberry loaf is perfect for breakfast, brunch, or as a delightful snack with tea or coffee.
- Store any leftover loaf in an airtight container at room temperature for a few days, or in the refrigerator for longer storage.
- The optional orange glaze adds a sweet and tangy finish to the loaf, but you can omit it if desired. Enjoy this delicious and festive loaf during the holiday season or any time of the year!

**Pistachio Macarons**

Ingredients:

*For the Macaron Shells:*

- 1 cup powdered sugar
- 3/4 cup almond flour
- 1/4 cup finely ground pistachios (from shelled pistachios)
- 2 large egg whites, at room temperature
- 1/4 cup granulated sugar
- Green food coloring (optional)

*For the Pistachio Filling:*

- 1/2 cup unsalted butter, softened
- 1 cup powdered sugar
- 1/4 cup finely ground pistachios (from shelled pistachios)
- 1-2 tablespoons heavy cream
- 1/2 teaspoon vanilla extract

Instructions:

Prepare Baking Sheets:
- Line two baking sheets with parchment paper or silicone mats. Have a piping bag ready fitted with a round tip.

Prepare Dry Ingredients:
- In a medium bowl, sift together the powdered sugar, almond flour, and finely ground pistachios. Set aside.

Whip Egg Whites:
- In a clean mixing bowl, beat the egg whites with an electric mixer on medium speed until foamy.
- Gradually add the granulated sugar while continuing to beat.
- Increase the speed to high and beat until stiff peaks form and the meringue is glossy. Add green food coloring if desired and mix until evenly colored.

Fold in Dry Ingredients:
- Gently fold the sifted dry ingredients into the meringue using a spatula, until the mixture is smooth and shiny. Be careful not to overmix.

Pipe Macaron Shells:
- Transfer the macaron batter into the prepared piping bag.
- Pipe small circles (about 1 inch in diameter) onto the prepared baking sheets, spacing them about 1 inch apart.

**Tap and Rest:**
- Tap the baking sheets on the counter a few times to release any air bubbles.
- Let the piped macarons rest at room temperature for 30-60 minutes, until a skin forms on the surface and they are no longer sticky to the touch.

**Preheat and Bake:**
- Preheat your oven to 300°F (150°C) while the macarons are resting.
- Bake the macarons, one sheet at a time, for 15-18 minutes, until set but not browned.
- Remove from the oven and let them cool completely on the baking sheets.

**Make Pistachio Filling:**
- In a mixing bowl, beat the softened butter until creamy.
- Gradually add the powdered sugar and finely ground pistachios, beating until smooth and fluffy.
- Add heavy cream and vanilla extract, adjusting the consistency as needed for easy piping.

**Assemble Macarons:**
- Match the cooled macaron shells into pairs of similar sizes.
- Pipe or spread a small amount of pistachio filling onto one shell of each pair.
- Sandwich with the remaining shells, pressing gently to adhere.

**Chill and Serve:**
- Place the assembled macarons in an airtight container and refrigerate for 24 hours to allow the flavors to meld.
- Bring to room temperature before serving. Enjoy these delicate and delicious pistachio macarons!

## Notes:

- Store leftover macarons in the refrigerator in an airtight container for up to 5 days. Bring them to room temperature before serving.
- Macarons can be a bit finicky, so practice and patience are key to achieving the perfect texture and shape.
- Experiment with different food colorings and flavorings for unique variations of these delightful pistachio macarons!

**Tea-Infused Truffles**

Ingredients:

- 1 cup heavy cream
- 2 tablespoons loose leaf tea (such as Earl Grey, jasmine, or chai)
- 12 ounces dark chocolate, finely chopped
- 2 tablespoons unsalted butter, softened
- Cocoa powder, powdered sugar, or finely chopped nuts for coating

Instructions:

Infuse the Cream:
- In a small saucepan, heat the heavy cream over medium heat until it just begins to simmer (do not boil).
- Remove from heat and add the loose leaf tea. Let it steep for about 5-10 minutes, depending on the desired strength of tea flavor.

Strain the Cream:
- Strain the infused cream through a fine-mesh sieve into a clean bowl, pressing on the tea leaves to extract maximum flavor. Discard the tea leaves.

Melt the Chocolate:
- Place the finely chopped dark chocolate in a heatproof bowl.
- In a small saucepan, reheat the infused cream just until simmering again.
- Pour the hot cream over the chopped chocolate. Let it sit for 1 minute, then gently stir until the chocolate is completely melted and smooth.

Incorporate Butter:
- Add the softened butter to the chocolate mixture and stir until fully incorporated and the mixture is glossy and smooth.

Chill the Ganache:
- Cover the chocolate ganache with plastic wrap, making sure the wrap touches the surface of the ganache to prevent a skin from forming.
- Refrigerate the ganache until firm, at least 2 hours or overnight.

Shape the Truffles:
- Once the ganache is firm, use a small spoon or melon baller to scoop out portions of the ganache and roll them into small balls with your hands.
- Place the truffles on a parchment-lined baking sheet. If the ganache gets too soft to handle, return it to the refrigerator to firm up.

Coat the Truffles:
- Roll each truffle in cocoa powder, powdered sugar, or finely chopped nuts, coating evenly.
- Gently shake off any excess coating and place the coated truffles back on the baking sheet.

Chill and Serve:

- Refrigerate the coated truffles for at least 30 minutes to set the coatings.
- Serve the tea-infused truffles chilled or at room temperature.

Notes:

- Experiment with different types of tea to create unique flavor combinations.
- Store the finished truffles in an airtight container in the refrigerator for up to 1 week.
- Bring the truffles to room temperature before serving to enjoy their rich and creamy texture. These tea-infused truffles make a delightful homemade treat or a thoughtful gift for tea lovers!

## Smoked Salmon Pinwheels

Ingredients:

- 8 ounces cream cheese, softened
- 1 tablespoon fresh dill, finely chopped (or 1 teaspoon dried dill)
- 1 tablespoon capers, drained and chopped
- Zest of 1 lemon
- Salt and black pepper, to taste
- 4 large flour tortillas (10-inch size)
- 8 ounces smoked salmon, thinly sliced
- 1 cup baby spinach leaves

Instructions:

Prepare the Cream Cheese Mixture:
- In a mixing bowl, combine the softened cream cheese, chopped dill, chopped capers, lemon zest, salt, and black pepper. Mix until smooth and well combined.

Assemble the Pinwheels:
- Lay out the flour tortillas on a clean work surface.
- Spread an even layer of the cream cheese mixture over each tortilla, covering all the way to the edges.

Layer with Smoked Salmon and Spinach:
- Arrange the thinly sliced smoked salmon evenly over the cream cheese layer on each tortilla.
- Top with a layer of baby spinach leaves.

Roll Up the Tortillas:
- Starting from one end, tightly roll up each tortilla into a log shape.

Slice into Pinwheels:
- Use a sharp knife to slice each rolled tortilla into 1-inch thick pinwheels.

Chill and Serve:
- Arrange the smoked salmon pinwheels on a serving platter.
- If not serving immediately, cover with plastic wrap and refrigerate until ready to serve.

Notes:

- Customize the filling by adding finely chopped red onion, cucumber slices, or avocado for additional flavors and textures.
- These smoked salmon pinwheels are perfect for parties, brunches, or as appetizers for any occasion.

- Feel free to use flavored tortillas (such as spinach or sun-dried tomato) for extra color and flavor.
- Serve the pinwheels chilled or at room temperature for best taste and texture. Enjoy these delicious and elegant smoked salmon pinwheels!

**Lavender Honey Cake**

Ingredients:

- 1/2 cup unsalted butter, softened
- 3/4 cup granulated sugar
- 2 large eggs
- 1 teaspoon vanilla extract
- 1/4 cup honey
- 1 tablespoon culinary lavender buds (dried or fresh)
- 1 1/2 cups all-purpose flour
- 1 1/2 teaspoons baking powder
- 1/4 teaspoon salt
- 1/2 cup milk
- Optional: Lavender glaze (see instructions below)

For the Lavender Glaze (Optional):

- 1 cup powdered sugar
- 2-3 tablespoons milk
- 1/2 teaspoon vanilla extract
- 1/2 teaspoon culinary lavender buds (dried or fresh), for decoration

Instructions:

Preheat the Oven and Prepare Pan:
- Preheat your oven to 350°F (175°C). Grease and flour a 9-inch round cake pan.

Cream Butter and Sugar:
- In a large mixing bowl, cream together the softened butter and granulated sugar until light and fluffy.

Add Eggs and Flavorings:
- Beat in the eggs, one at a time, until well combined.
- Mix in the vanilla extract and honey.

Infuse with Lavender:
- In a small saucepan, heat the milk until steaming (but not boiling). Remove from heat and stir in the culinary lavender buds. Let it steep for about 10 minutes to infuse the milk with lavender flavor. Strain out the lavender buds and allow the milk to cool slightly.

Combine Dry Ingredients:
- In a separate bowl, whisk together the flour, baking powder, and salt.

Alternate Mixing:
- Gradually add the dry ingredients to the creamed butter mixture, alternating with the lavender-infused milk, beginning and ending with the dry ingredients. Mix until just combined.

Bake the Cake:
- Pour the batter into the prepared cake pan and smooth the top with a spatula.
- Bake in the preheated oven for 25-30 minutes, or until a toothpick inserted into the center comes out clean.

Cool and Prepare Glaze (Optional):
- Allow the cake to cool in the pan for 10 minutes, then transfer it to a wire rack to cool completely.
- If making the lavender glaze, whisk together the powdered sugar, milk, and vanilla extract until smooth. Drizzle the glaze over the cooled cake and sprinkle with culinary lavender buds for decoration.

Serve and Enjoy:
- Slice the lavender honey cake and serve at room temperature.

Notes:

- Culinary lavender buds can be found at specialty food stores or online. Ensure you are using culinary lavender specifically meant for consumption.
- Adjust the amount of lavender according to your preference for intensity of flavor.
- This lavender honey cake is delightful with a cup of tea or coffee, perfect for special occasions or as a unique dessert. Enjoy the delicate floral notes and honey sweetness in every bite!

## Cheddar and Chive Biscuits

Ingredients:

- 2 cups all-purpose flour
- 1 tablespoon baking powder
- 1/2 teaspoon baking soda
- 1 teaspoon salt
- 1/2 cup unsalted butter, cold and cubed
- 1 cup grated sharp cheddar cheese
- 1/4 cup chopped fresh chives
- 3/4 cup buttermilk (or milk with a splash of vinegar)
- 1 large egg, beaten (for egg wash)

Instructions:

Preheat the Oven:
- Preheat your oven to 425°F (220°C). Line a baking sheet with parchment paper.

Prepare Dry Ingredients:
- In a large bowl, whisk together the flour, baking powder, baking soda, and salt.

Cut in Butter:
- Add the cold cubed butter to the flour mixture.
- Use a pastry cutter or your fingers to work the butter into the flour until the mixture resembles coarse crumbs.

Add Cheese and Chives:
- Stir in the grated cheddar cheese and chopped fresh chives until evenly distributed in the flour mixture.

Combine Wet Ingredients:
- Make a well in the center of the flour mixture.
- Pour in the buttermilk (or milk with vinegar).
- Use a fork or spatula to gently mix the wet and dry ingredients together until a dough forms. Be careful not to overmix.

Shape and Cut Biscuits:
- Transfer the dough onto a lightly floured surface.
- Pat the dough into a rectangle about 1-inch thick.
- Use a sharp knife or biscuit cutter to cut out rounds of dough (about 2.5 inches in diameter) and place them on the prepared baking sheet, spacing them slightly apart.

Brush with Egg Wash:
- Brush the tops of the biscuits with the beaten egg.

Bake the Biscuits:
- Bake in the preheated oven for 12-15 minutes, or until the biscuits are golden brown and cooked through.

Cool and Serve:
- Remove the biscuits from the oven and let them cool on the baking sheet for a few minutes.
- Serve the cheddar and chive biscuits warm. Enjoy them as a side dish or snack!

Notes:

- These biscuits are best enjoyed fresh and warm from the oven.
- Store any leftover biscuits in an airtight container at room temperature for up to 2 days. Reheat briefly in the oven or microwave before serving.
- Feel free to customize these biscuits by adding other herbs or spices, such as garlic powder or black pepper, for additional flavor variations.
- Serve these savory cheddar and chive biscuits alongside soups, salads, or as part of a brunch spread. They are deliciously cheesy and packed with fresh herb flavor!

**Strawberry Cream Puffs**

Ingredients:

*For the Cream Puffs:*

- 1/2 cup unsalted butter
- 1 cup water
- 1/4 teaspoon salt
- 1 cup all-purpose flour
- 4 large eggs

*For the Strawberry Filling:*

- 1 pound fresh strawberries, hulled and sliced
- 1/2 cup granulated sugar
- 1 cup heavy cream
- 2 tablespoons powdered sugar
- 1 teaspoon vanilla extract

Instructions:

Prepare the Strawberry Filling:
- In a mixing bowl, combine the sliced strawberries with granulated sugar. Let them macerate for at least 30 minutes to release juices and soften.

Make the Cream Puffs:
- Preheat your oven to 400°F (200°C). Line a baking sheet with parchment paper.
- In a medium saucepan, combine the butter, water, and salt. Bring to a boil over medium heat.
- Add the flour all at once and stir vigorously with a wooden spoon until the mixture forms a ball and pulls away from the sides of the pan.
- Remove from heat and let cool for 5 minutes.
- Add the eggs, one at a time, stirring well after each addition until fully incorporated and the dough is smooth and glossy.

Pipe and Bake the Cream Puffs:
- Transfer the dough to a piping bag fitted with a large round tip (or use a spoon). Pipe 1 1/2-inch mounds of dough onto the prepared baking sheet, spacing them about 2 inches apart.
- Bake in the preheated oven for 20-25 minutes or until puffed and golden brown.
- Remove from the oven and let the cream puffs cool completely on a wire rack.

Prepare the Whipped Cream:

- In a chilled mixing bowl, whip the heavy cream with powdered sugar and vanilla extract until stiff peaks form.

Assemble the Strawberry Cream Puffs:
- Cut the tops off of the cooled cream puffs.
- Fill each puff with a spoonful of macerated strawberries.
- Pipe or spoon whipped cream over the strawberries.

Serve and Enjoy:
- Place the tops back on the filled cream puffs.
- Dust with powdered sugar if desired.
- Serve immediately and enjoy these delightful strawberry cream puffs!

Notes:

- The cream puffs are best assembled and served fresh for optimal texture.
- You can customize the filling by adding a layer of strawberry jam or a drizzle of chocolate ganache.
- Store any leftover assembled cream puffs in the refrigerator for up to 1 day. Assemble just before serving for the best results.

**Lemon Tartlets**

Ingredients:

*For the Tartlet Shells:*

- 1 1/4 cups all-purpose flour
- 1/4 cup granulated sugar
- 1/4 teaspoon salt
- 1/2 cup unsalted butter, cold and cubed
- 1 large egg yolk
- 1-2 tablespoons ice water

*For the Lemon Curd Filling:*

- 3/4 cup granulated sugar
- Zest of 2 lemons
- 1/2 cup freshly squeezed lemon juice (from about 2-3 lemons)
- 4 large egg yolks
- 6 tablespoons unsalted butter, cut into small pieces

Instructions:

Make the Tartlet Shells:
- In a food processor, combine the flour, sugar, and salt. Pulse a few times to mix.
- Add the cold cubed butter and pulse until the mixture resembles coarse crumbs.
- In a small bowl, whisk together the egg yolk and 1 tablespoon of ice water. Drizzle this mixture into the food processor while pulsing, just until the dough starts to come together.
- If needed, add an additional tablespoon of ice water, one teaspoon at a time, until the dough forms a ball.
- Turn out the dough onto a lightly floured surface and shape it into a disc. Wrap in plastic wrap and refrigerate for at least 30 minutes.

Preheat the Oven:
- Preheat your oven to 375°F (190°C).

Roll Out and Shape the Tartlet Shells:
- On a lightly floured surface, roll out the chilled dough to about 1/8-inch thickness.
- Using a round cookie cutter or a glass, cut out circles of dough slightly larger than the indentations in your mini tartlet pans.
- Gently press the dough circles into the mini tartlet pans, trimming any excess dough from the edges.

Blind Bake the Tartlet Shells:

- Prick the bottom of each tartlet shell with a fork.
- Line each tartlet shell with parchment paper and fill with pie weights or dried beans.
- Bake in the preheated oven for 12-15 minutes, or until the edges are golden brown.
- Remove the parchment paper and weights, and bake for an additional 3-4 minutes until the bottom of the shells are fully baked and golden.
- Remove from the oven and let the tartlet shells cool completely in the pans.

Make the Lemon Curd Filling:
- In a heatproof bowl set over a pot of simmering water (double boiler method), whisk together the sugar, lemon zest, lemon juice, and egg yolks.
- Cook the mixture, whisking constantly, until it thickens and coats the back of a spoon (about 8-10 minutes).
- Remove from heat and whisk in the butter, a few pieces at a time, until smooth and incorporated.

Fill the Tartlet Shells:
- Spoon the lemon curd filling into the cooled tartlet shells, smoothing the tops with a spatula.

Chill and Serve:
- Refrigerate the lemon tartlets for at least 1-2 hours to set the filling.
- Before serving, garnish with additional lemon zest or whipped cream if desired.

Notes:

- These lemon tartlets are perfect for parties, afternoon tea, or any special occasion.
- Store any leftover tartlets in the refrigerator in an airtight container for up to 3 days.
- Feel free to garnish with fresh berries or a dusting of powdered sugar before serving.
- Enjoy these delightful and tangy lemon tartlets as a refreshing dessert!

**Mini Pavlovas with Berries**

Ingredients:

*For the Mini Pavlovas:*

- 4 large egg whites, at room temperature
- 1 cup granulated sugar
- 1 teaspoon cornstarch
- 1 teaspoon white vinegar
- 1/2 teaspoon vanilla extract

*For the Topping:*

- 1 cup heavy cream, cold
- 2 tablespoons powdered sugar
- 1 teaspoon vanilla extract
- Assorted fresh berries (such as strawberries, blueberries, raspberries)

Instructions:

Preheat the Oven:
- Preheat your oven to 250°F (120°C). Line a baking sheet with parchment paper.

Prepare the Mini Pavlovas:
- In a clean mixing bowl, beat the egg whites with an electric mixer on medium speed until soft peaks form.
- Gradually add the granulated sugar, about 1 tablespoon at a time, while continuing to beat.
- Once all the sugar is added, increase the mixer speed to high and continue beating until stiff peaks form and the meringue is glossy.
- Gently fold in the cornstarch, white vinegar, and vanilla extract until fully incorporated.

Shape and Bake the Pavlovas:
- Spoon or pipe the meringue onto the prepared baking sheet to form mini pavlovas (about 3-4 inches in diameter), leaving a slight indentation in the center of each.
- Use the back of a spoon to create a swirl or decorative pattern around the edges of the pavlovas.

Bake and Cool:
- Place the baking sheet in the preheated oven and immediately reduce the temperature to 225°F (110°C).

- Bake the mini pavlovas for 60-75 minutes, or until they are dry to the touch and lightly golden.
- Turn off the oven and let the pavlovas cool completely inside the oven with the door slightly ajar.

Prepare the Whipped Cream:
- In a chilled mixing bowl, whip the cold heavy cream with powdered sugar and vanilla extract until stiff peaks form.

Assemble the Mini Pavlovas:
- Gently remove the cooled mini pavlovas from the parchment paper.
- Spoon a dollop of whipped cream into the center of each pavlova.
- Top with assorted fresh berries, arranging them attractively on top of the whipped cream.

Serve and Enjoy:
- Serve the mini pavlovas with berries immediately, as they are best enjoyed fresh.

Notes:

- Mini pavlovas can be made ahead of time and stored in an airtight container at room temperature for up to 2 days.
- Assemble the pavlovas with whipped cream and berries just before serving to prevent them from becoming soggy.
- Feel free to drizzle with honey or sprinkle with powdered sugar for extra sweetness.
- Enjoy these elegant and light mini pavlovas with a delightful combination of crunchy meringue, creamy whipped cream, and fresh berries!

**Spinach and Feta Triangles**

Ingredients:

- 1 tablespoon olive oil
- 1 small onion, finely chopped
- 2 cloves garlic, minced
- 10 ounces frozen chopped spinach, thawed and squeezed dry
- 4 ounces feta cheese, crumbled
- 1/4 cup grated Parmesan cheese
- Salt and pepper, to taste
- Pinch of nutmeg (optional)
- 1 package (about 16 ounces) phyllo dough, thawed
- 1/2 cup (1 stick) unsalted butter, melted

Instructions:

Prepare the Spinach Filling:
- Heat olive oil in a skillet over medium heat. Add chopped onion and sauté until translucent, about 3-4 minutes.
- Add minced garlic and cook for another 1-2 minutes until fragrant.
- Stir in the thawed and squeezed dry chopped spinach. Cook for 2-3 minutes to combine flavors.
- Remove from heat and let the mixture cool slightly.
- Transfer the spinach mixture to a mixing bowl and stir in crumbled feta cheese, grated Parmesan cheese, salt, pepper, and a pinch of nutmeg (if using). Set aside.

Prepare the Phyllo Dough:
- Preheat your oven to 375°F (190°C). Line a baking sheet with parchment paper.
- Carefully unroll the thawed phyllo dough sheets on a clean, dry surface. Cover the sheets with a damp kitchen towel to prevent drying out.

Assemble the Triangles:
- Take one sheet of phyllo dough and brush it lightly with melted butter.
- Place another sheet of phyllo dough on top and brush with melted butter.
- Cut the double-layered phyllo dough into strips about 3 inches wide (you should get about 4-5 strips from each double-layered sheet).

Fill and Fold the Triangles:
- Place a spoonful of the spinach and feta filling at one end of each strip.

- Fold one corner of the strip over the filling to form a triangle, then continue folding the triangle (like folding a flag) until you reach the end of the strip.
- Brush the outside of each folded triangle with melted butter and place it seam-side down on the prepared baking sheet.
- Repeat the process with the remaining phyllo dough strips and filling.

Bake the Triangles:
- Bake in the preheated oven for 12-15 minutes, or until the triangles are golden brown and crisp.

Serve and Enjoy:
- Remove the spinach and feta triangles from the oven and let them cool slightly before serving.
- Serve warm as an appetizer or snack.

Notes:

- Make sure to thaw the phyllo dough according to package instructions and work quickly with the dough, as it can dry out easily.
- These spinach and feta triangles can be made ahead of time and frozen before baking. Simply arrange the filled triangles on a baking sheet, freeze until firm, then transfer to a freezer bag. Bake from frozen, adding a few extra minutes to the baking time.
- Feel free to customize the filling with additional herbs or spices, such as dill or red pepper flakes, for extra flavor variations.
- Enjoy these delicious and crispy spinach and feta triangles as a flavorful appetizer or party snack!

**Chocolate Chip Cookies**

Ingredients:

- 1 cup (2 sticks) unsalted butter, softened
- 3/4 cup granulated sugar
- 3/4 cup packed light brown sugar
- 2 large eggs
- 1 teaspoon vanilla extract
- 2 1/4 cups all-purpose flour
- 1 teaspoon baking soda
- 1/2 teaspoon salt
- 2 cups semi-sweet chocolate chips

Instructions:

Preheat the Oven:
- Preheat your oven to 375°F (190°C). Line baking sheets with parchment paper or silicone baking mats.

Cream Butter and Sugars:
- In a large mixing bowl, beat together the softened butter, granulated sugar, and brown sugar until creamy and well combined.

Add Eggs and Vanilla:
- Add the eggs one at a time, beating well after each addition.
- Stir in the vanilla extract.

Combine Dry Ingredients:
- In a separate bowl, whisk together the flour, baking soda, and salt.

Mix the Dough:
- Gradually add the dry ingredients to the wet ingredients, mixing until just combined.
- Stir in the chocolate chips until evenly distributed throughout the dough.

Scoop and Bake:
- Drop rounded tablespoonfuls of dough onto the prepared baking sheets, spacing them about 2 inches apart.

Bake the Cookies:
- Bake in the preheated oven for 9-11 minutes, or until the edges are golden brown.
- The centers may still look slightly soft.
- Remove from the oven and let the cookies cool on the baking sheets for a few minutes before transferring them to wire racks to cool completely.

Enjoy:
- Once cooled, enjoy these classic chocolate chip cookies with a glass of milk or your favorite beverage!

Notes:

- For chewier cookies, slightly underbake them and let them finish setting up on the baking sheet after removing from the oven.
- You can customize these cookies by using different types of chocolate chips (such as milk chocolate or dark chocolate) or adding nuts like chopped walnuts or pecans.
- Store leftover cookies in an airtight container at room temperature for up to one week, or freeze for longer storage.
- Feel free to double the recipe if you want to make a larger batch of delicious homemade chocolate chip cookies!

**Carrot Cake Cupcakes**

Ingredients:

*For the Cupcakes:*

- 1 cup all-purpose flour
- 1 teaspoon baking powder
- 1/2 teaspoon baking soda
- 1/2 teaspoon salt
- 1 teaspoon ground cinnamon
- 1/2 teaspoon ground ginger
- 1/4 teaspoon ground nutmeg
- 2 large eggs
- 3/4 cup granulated sugar
- 1/2 cup vegetable oil
- 1 teaspoon vanilla extract
- 1 1/2 cups finely grated carrots (about 2-3 medium carrots)
- 1/2 cup crushed pineapple, drained (optional)
- 1/2 cup chopped walnuts or pecans (optional)
- 1/4 cup shredded coconut (optional)

*For the Cream Cheese Frosting:*

- 8 ounces cream cheese, softened
- 1/4 cup unsalted butter, softened
- 2 cups powdered sugar
- 1 teaspoon vanilla extract

Instructions:

Preheat the Oven:
- Preheat your oven to 350°F (175°C). Line a muffin tin with cupcake liners.

Prepare the Dry Ingredients:
- In a mixing bowl, whisk together the flour, baking powder, baking soda, salt, cinnamon, ginger, and nutmeg until well combined. Set aside.

Mix the Wet Ingredients:
- In a separate large mixing bowl, beat the eggs and granulated sugar until pale and creamy.
- Add the vegetable oil and vanilla extract, and mix until well combined.

Combine Wet and Dry Ingredients:

- Gradually add the dry ingredients to the wet ingredients, mixing until just combined.
- Fold in the grated carrots, crushed pineapple (if using), chopped nuts (if using), and shredded coconut (if using), until evenly distributed in the batter.

Fill the Cupcake Liners:
- Spoon the batter into the prepared cupcake liners, filling each about 2/3 full.

Bake the Cupcakes:
- Bake in the preheated oven for 18-20 minutes, or until a toothpick inserted into the center comes out clean.
- Remove from the oven and let the cupcakes cool in the pan for a few minutes before transferring them to a wire rack to cool completely.

Prepare the Cream Cheese Frosting:
- In a mixing bowl, beat together the softened cream cheese and butter until smooth and creamy.
- Add the powdered sugar and vanilla extract, and continue beating until the frosting is smooth and fluffy.

Frost the Cupcakes:
- Once the cupcakes are completely cooled, frost them with the cream cheese frosting using a piping bag or spread it with a knife.

Decorate and Serve:
- Optionally, garnish with additional chopped nuts or a sprinkle of cinnamon on top.
- Serve and enjoy these delicious carrot cake cupcakes!

Notes:

- You can customize these cupcakes by adding or omitting optional ingredients like pineapple, nuts, and coconut based on your preference.
- Store leftover cupcakes in an airtight container in the refrigerator for up to 4-5 days.
- Bring cupcakes to room temperature before serving for the best taste and texture.
- These carrot cake cupcakes are perfect for parties, gatherings, or as a sweet treat any time of the year!

**Elderflower Cupcakes**

Ingredients:

*For the Cupcakes:*

- 1 1/2 cups all-purpose flour
- 1 1/2 teaspoons baking powder
- 1/4 teaspoon salt
- 1/2 cup (1 stick) unsalted butter, softened
- 1 cup granulated sugar
- 2 large eggs
- 1 teaspoon vanilla extract
- 1/2 cup milk
- 2 tablespoons elderflower cordial

*For the Elderflower Buttercream:*

- 1/2 cup (1 stick) unsalted butter, softened
- 2 cups powdered sugar
- 2-3 tablespoons elderflower cordial
- Edible flowers or elderflower blossoms (for decoration, optional)

Instructions:

Preheat the Oven:
- Preheat your oven to 350°F (175°C). Line a muffin tin with cupcake liners.

Prepare the Dry Ingredients:
- In a mixing bowl, whisk together the flour, baking powder, and salt. Set aside.

Cream Butter and Sugar:
- In a separate large mixing bowl, cream together the softened butter and granulated sugar until light and fluffy.

Add Eggs and Vanilla:
- Beat in the eggs, one at a time, until well combined.
- Stir in the vanilla extract.

Combine Wet and Dry Ingredients:
- Gradually add the dry ingredients to the wet ingredients, alternating with the milk, beginning and ending with the dry ingredients.
- Mix until just combined, being careful not to overmix.

Add Elderflower Cordial:
- Stir in the elderflower cordial until incorporated into the cupcake batter.

Fill Cupcake Liners:
- Divide the batter evenly among the prepared cupcake liners, filling each about 2/3 full.

Bake the Cupcakes:
- Bake in the preheated oven for 18-20 minutes, or until a toothpick inserted into the center comes out clean.
- Remove from the oven and let the cupcakes cool in the pan for a few minutes before transferring them to a wire rack to cool completely.

Prepare the Elderflower Buttercream:
- In a mixing bowl, beat the softened butter until creamy.
- Gradually add the powdered sugar, one cup at a time, beating well after each addition.
- Add elderflower cordial, starting with 2 tablespoons and adding more as needed for desired flavor and consistency.

Frost the Cupcakes:
- Once the cupcakes are completely cooled, frost them with the elderflower buttercream using a piping bag or spread it with a knife.

Decorate and Serve:
- Optionally, decorate each cupcake with edible flowers or elderflower blossoms for a beautiful presentation.
- Serve and enjoy these delightful elderflower cupcakes!

Notes:

- Elderflower cordial can be found in specialty grocery stores or online. If you cannot find elderflower cordial, you can substitute with elderflower syrup or concentrate.
- Store leftover cupcakes in an airtight container in the refrigerator for up to 3-4 days.
- Bring cupcakes to room temperature before serving for the best taste and texture.
- These elderflower cupcakes are perfect for spring or summer gatherings and celebrations!

**Almond Crescents**

Ingredients:

- 1 cup unsalted butter, softened
- 1/2 cup granulated sugar
- 1 teaspoon vanilla extract
- 1 teaspoon almond extract
- 2 cups all-purpose flour
- 1 cup finely ground almonds (almond flour)
- 1/4 teaspoon salt
- Powdered sugar, for dusting

Instructions:

Preheat the Oven:
- Preheat your oven to 350°F (175°C). Line a baking sheet with parchment paper.

Cream Butter and Sugar:
- In a mixing bowl, cream together the softened butter and granulated sugar until light and fluffy.

Add Extracts:
- Stir in the vanilla extract and almond extract until well combined.

Combine Dry Ingredients:
- In a separate bowl, whisk together the all-purpose flour, ground almonds (almond flour), and salt.

Mix the Dough:
- Gradually add the dry ingredients to the butter mixture, mixing until a dough forms.
- The dough should be smooth and slightly sticky.

Shape the Crescents:
- Take small portions of the dough and shape them into crescent shapes. Roll each portion into a ball, then gently roll it between your palms to form a log shape.
- Curve the log into a crescent shape and place it on the prepared baking sheet.
- Repeat with the remaining dough, spacing the crescents about 1 inch apart on the baking sheet.

Bake the Crescents:

- Bake in the preheated oven for 12-15 minutes, or until the bottoms are lightly golden.
- Remove from the oven and let the crescents cool on the baking sheet for a few minutes before transferring them to a wire rack to cool completely.

Dust with Powdered Sugar:
- Once the almond crescents are completely cooled, dust them generously with powdered sugar.

Serve and Enjoy:
- Arrange the almond crescents on a serving platter and enjoy with a cup of tea or coffee.

Notes:

- You can optionally add a sprinkle of finely chopped almonds on top of the crescents before baking for extra texture.
- Store leftover almond crescents in an airtight container at room temperature for up to one week.
- These almond crescents make a delightful treat for holidays, parties, or afternoon tea gatherings. They have a lovely almond flavor and a delicate texture that melts in your mouth!

**Tea-Infused Panna Cotta**

Ingredients:

- 2 cups heavy cream
- 1 cup whole milk
- 1/2 cup granulated sugar
- 2 tablespoons loose leaf tea (such as Earl Grey, jasmine, or green tea)
- 1 teaspoon vanilla extract
- 2 packets (14 grams) powdered gelatin
- 1/4 cup cold water
- Fresh berries or fruit, for serving (optional)

Instructions:

Infuse the Cream and Milk:
- In a saucepan, combine the heavy cream, whole milk, and granulated sugar over medium heat.
- Add the loose leaf tea to the cream mixture and stir gently.
- Heat the mixture until it starts to simmer, then remove from heat. Cover and let steep for about 15-20 minutes to infuse the flavors.

Strain the Mixture:
- After steeping, strain the cream mixture through a fine-mesh sieve or cheesecloth to remove the tea leaves.
- Return the infused cream mixture to the saucepan and place it back over low heat to keep warm.

Bloom the Gelatin:
- In a small bowl, sprinkle the powdered gelatin over the cold water. Let it sit for about 5 minutes to bloom and soften.

Combine Gelatin with Cream Mixture:
- Once the gelatin has bloomed, add it to the warm cream mixture in the saucepan.
- Stir gently until the gelatin is completely dissolved and incorporated into the cream mixture.
- Remove from heat and stir in the vanilla extract.

Pour into Serving Containers:
- Divide the tea-infused panna cotta mixture evenly among serving glasses or molds.
- Refrigerate for at least 4 hours, or until set and firm.

Serve and Enjoy:
- Once set, garnish the tea-infused panna cotta with fresh berries or fruit, if desired.
- Serve chilled and enjoy this elegant and creamy dessert with delightful tea flavors!

Notes:

- You can use any type of loose leaf tea you prefer for infusing the cream mixture. Experiment with different tea varieties to create unique flavors.
- Make sure to strain the mixture well after steeping to remove all the tea leaves and achieve a smooth texture in the panna cotta.
- If you prefer a sweeter panna cotta, you can adjust the amount of sugar to taste.
- This tea-infused panna cotta is perfect for serving at tea parties, special occasions, or as a sophisticated dessert after dinner. The delicate tea flavor adds a lovely touch to this creamy treat!

**Apricot Rugelach**

Ingredients:

*For the Dough:*

- 1 cup unsalted butter, softened
- 8 ounces cream cheese, softened
- 2 cups all-purpose flour
- 1/4 teaspoon salt
- 1/4 cup granulated sugar
- 1 teaspoon vanilla extract

*For the Filling:*

- 1 cup apricot preserves
- 1/2 cup chopped walnuts or pecans
- 1/4 cup granulated sugar
- 1 teaspoon ground cinnamon
- 1/4 teaspoon ground nutmeg
- Egg wash (1 egg beaten with 1 tablespoon water)
- Powdered sugar, for dusting (optional)

Instructions:

Prepare the Dough:
- In a large mixing bowl, cream together the softened butter and cream cheese until smooth and well combined.
- Add the flour, salt, granulated sugar, and vanilla extract to the bowl. Mix until the dough comes together and forms a ball.
- Divide the dough into 4 equal portions, shape each portion into a disk, wrap in plastic wrap, and refrigerate for at least 1 hour (or up to overnight).

Make the Filling:
- In a small bowl, mix together the apricot preserves, chopped nuts, granulated sugar, cinnamon, and nutmeg. Set aside.

Assemble the Rugelach:
- Preheat your oven to 350°F (175°C). Line baking sheets with parchment paper.
- Remove one portion of dough from the refrigerator and roll it out on a lightly floured surface into a circle, about 1/8 inch thick.
- Spread a quarter of the apricot filling evenly over the dough circle, leaving a small border around the edges.

- Use a pizza cutter or sharp knife to cut the dough circle into 12 equal wedges (like cutting a pizza).

Roll Up the Rugelach:
- Starting from the wide edge of each wedge, roll up the dough towards the point to form a crescent shape.
- Place the rugelach, seam-side down, on the prepared baking sheet.
- Repeat with the remaining dough and filling.

Brush with Egg Wash:
- Brush the tops of the rugelach with the egg wash, which will give them a golden finish when baked.

Bake the Rugelach:
- Bake in the preheated oven for 20-25 minutes, or until golden brown and slightly puffed.
- Remove from the oven and let cool on the baking sheets for a few minutes before transferring to wire racks to cool completely.

Dust with Powdered Sugar:
- Once cooled, dust the apricot rugelach with powdered sugar, if desired.

Serve and Enjoy:
- Arrange the apricot rugelach on a serving platter and enjoy as a delightful treat with tea or coffee!

Notes:

- You can customize the filling by using different fruit preserves (such as raspberry or strawberry) or adding chocolate chips or raisins to the filling mixture.
- Store leftover rugelach in an airtight container at room temperature for up to 3-4 days, or freeze for longer storage.
- Apricot rugelach is a classic pastry that's perfect for holidays, parties, or any occasion. These flaky, fruity treats are sure to be a hit with family and friends!

**Mini Tarts with Fruit Compote**

Ingredients:

*For the Tart Crust:*

- 1 1/4 cups all-purpose flour
- 1/4 cup granulated sugar
- 1/4 teaspoon salt
- 1/2 cup unsalted butter, cold and cut into small pieces
- 1 large egg yolk
- 2 tablespoons ice water

*For the Fruit Compote:*

- 2 cups fresh or frozen mixed berries (such as strawberries, blueberries, raspberries)
- 1/4 cup granulated sugar
- 1 tablespoon lemon juice
- 1 tablespoon cornstarch dissolved in 1 tablespoon water

*For Assembly:*

- Fresh berries for topping
- Powdered sugar, for dusting (optional)

Instructions:

Make the Tart Crust:
- In a food processor, pulse together the flour, sugar, and salt until combined.
- Add the cold butter and pulse until the mixture resembles coarse crumbs.
- In a small bowl, whisk together the egg yolk and ice water.
- With the food processor running, gradually add the egg mixture until the dough comes together.
- Turn the dough out onto a lightly floured surface and gently knead until smooth.
- Flatten the dough into a disk, wrap in plastic wrap, and refrigerate for at least 30 minutes.

Prepare the Fruit Compote:
- In a saucepan, combine the mixed berries, granulated sugar, and lemon juice over medium heat.
- Cook, stirring occasionally, until the berries release their juices and the mixture begins to simmer.

- Stir in the cornstarch mixture and continue to cook until the compote thickens, about 2-3 minutes.
- Remove from heat and let cool completely.

Preheat the Oven:
- Preheat your oven to 375°F (190°C). Grease a mini tart pan with removable bottoms or mini muffin tins.

Roll Out the Dough:
- On a lightly floured surface, roll out the chilled dough to about 1/8 inch thick.
- Cut out circles slightly larger than the size of your tart or muffin tin cavities.

Line the Tart Pans:
- Gently press the dough circles into each cavity of the tart pan or muffin tin, ensuring the dough reaches up the sides.

Fill with Fruit Compote:
- Spoon a small amount of the cooled fruit compote into each tart shell, filling them just below the rim.

Bake the Tarts:
- Place the filled tart pans on a baking sheet and bake in the preheated oven for 12-15 minutes, or until the tart crusts are golden brown.
- Remove from the oven and let cool in the pans for a few minutes before carefully removing the tarts and transferring them to a wire rack to cool completely.

Assemble and Serve:
- Once cooled, top each mini tart with fresh berries and dust with powdered sugar, if desired.
- Serve these delightful mini tarts with fruit compote as a sweet and elegant dessert for any occasion!

Notes:

- You can use any combination of fresh or frozen berries for the fruit compote, depending on your preference and availability.
- These mini tarts can be made ahead of time and stored in an airtight container in the refrigerator. Serve them chilled or at room temperature.
- Experiment with different fruits and toppings to create variations of these delicious mini tarts to suit your taste!

**Cheese Straws**

Ingredients:

- 1 1/2 cups shredded sharp cheddar cheese
- 1/2 cup unsalted butter, softened
- 1 1/2 cups all-purpose flour
- 1/2 teaspoon salt
- 1/4 teaspoon cayenne pepper (optional, for a bit of heat)
- 1/4 teaspoon paprika
- 2 tablespoons cold water

Instructions:

Preheat the Oven:
- Preheat your oven to 375°F (190°C). Line a baking sheet with parchment paper.

Mix Ingredients:
- In a mixing bowl, combine the shredded cheddar cheese and softened butter.
- Add the flour, salt, cayenne pepper (if using), and paprika. Mix until the dough begins to come together.
- If the dough seems dry, add the cold water a little at a time until the dough holds together when pressed.

Form the Dough:
- Turn the dough out onto a lightly floured surface and knead gently until smooth.

Roll Out the Dough:
- Roll the dough out to about 1/4 inch thickness using a rolling pin.

Cut into Strips:
- Use a sharp knife or a pastry cutter to cut the dough into thin strips, about 1/2 inch wide and 4-5 inches long.

Twist the Straws:
- Gently twist each strip of dough a few times to create a twisted shape.

Bake the Cheese Straws:
- Place the twisted cheese straws on the prepared baking sheet, spacing them slightly apart.

**Bake in the preheated oven for 10-12 minutes, or until golden brown and crispy.

Cool and Serve:
- Remove from the oven and let the cheese straws cool on the baking sheet for a few minutes before transferring them to a wire rack to cool completely.
- Serve the cheese straws warm or at room temperature as a delicious snack or appetizer.

Notes:

- Feel free to customize the seasonings by adding herbs like thyme or rosemary, or adjusting the amount of cayenne pepper for spicier cheese straws.
- Store leftover cheese straws in an airtight container at room temperature for up to 3-4 days. You can also freeze them for longer storage and reheat in the oven before serving.
- Cheese straws are perfect for parties, gatherings, or as a tasty accompaniment to soups and salads. Enjoy their crispy, cheesy goodness!

**Walnut and Date Bars**

Ingredients:

- 1 cup pitted dates, chopped
- 1 cup walnuts, chopped
- 1/2 cup unsalted butter, melted
- 1/4 cup granulated sugar
- 1/4 cup brown sugar
- 1 large egg, lightly beaten
- 1 teaspoon vanilla extract
- 1 cup all-purpose flour
- 1/4 teaspoon salt
- Powdered sugar, for dusting (optional)

Instructions:

Preheat the Oven:
- Preheat your oven to 350°F (175°C). Grease or line a baking pan (8x8 inch) with parchment paper.

Prepare the Date and Walnut Mixture:
- In a bowl, combine the chopped dates and walnuts. Set aside.

Make the Batter:
- In a separate mixing bowl, whisk together the melted butter, granulated sugar, and brown sugar until well combined.
- Add the lightly beaten egg and vanilla extract, and mix until smooth.

Combine Dry Ingredients:
- In another bowl, whisk together the all-purpose flour and salt.

Mix Everything Together:
- Gradually add the flour mixture to the wet ingredients, stirring until just combined.
- Fold in the chopped dates and walnuts until evenly distributed in the batter.

Assemble and Bake:
- Spread the batter evenly into the prepared baking pan, smoothing the top with a spatula.

**Bake in the preheated oven for 20-25 minutes, or until the edges are golden brown and a toothpick inserted into the center comes out clean.

Cool and Cut:

- Allow the bars to cool completely in the pan on a wire rack.
- Once cooled, lift the bars out of the pan using the parchment paper and place on a cutting board.
- Cut into squares or bars of your desired size.

Dust with Powdered Sugar (Optional):
- If desired, dust the walnut and date bars with powdered sugar before serving.

Serve and Enjoy:
- Serve these delicious walnut and date bars as a snack or dessert. Store any leftovers in an airtight container at room temperature for a few days.

Notes:

- You can customize these bars by adding other ingredients such as chocolate chips, dried cranberries, or coconut flakes.
- Make sure to chop the dates and walnuts finely for even distribution throughout the bars.
- These bars are perfect for enjoying with a cup of coffee or tea, and they also make a great addition to dessert platters or gift baskets during the holidays. Enjoy the sweet and nutty flavors!

**Lemon Poppy Seed Muffins**

Ingredients:

- 2 cups all-purpose flour
- 1/2 cup granulated sugar
- 2 tablespoons poppy seeds
- 2 teaspoons baking powder
- 1/2 teaspoon baking soda
- 1/4 teaspoon salt
- 1 cup plain yogurt or Greek yogurt
- 1/2 cup unsalted butter, melted and slightly cooled
- 2 large eggs
- Zest of 2 lemons
- Juice of 1 lemon
- 1 teaspoon vanilla extract

For the Glaze (Optional):

- 1 cup powdered sugar
- 2-3 tablespoons fresh lemon juice

Instructions:

Preheat the Oven:
- Preheat your oven to 375°F (190°C). Line a muffin tin with paper liners or grease the muffin cups.

Mix Dry Ingredients:
- In a large bowl, whisk together the flour, sugar, poppy seeds, baking powder, baking soda, and salt.

Prepare Wet Ingredients:
- In another bowl, whisk together the yogurt, melted butter, eggs, lemon zest, lemon juice, and vanilla extract until smooth.

Combine Wet and Dry Ingredients:
- Pour the wet ingredients into the bowl of dry ingredients.
- Gently fold the mixture together with a spatula or wooden spoon until just combined. Do not overmix; a few lumps are okay.

Fill Muffin Cups:
- Divide the batter evenly among the prepared muffin cups, filling each about 3/4 full.

Bake the Muffins:

- Bake in the preheated oven for 18-20 minutes, or until the tops are golden brown and a toothpick inserted into the center comes out clean.

Cool Muffins:
- Allow the muffins to cool in the pan for 5 minutes, then transfer them to a wire rack to cool completely.

Make the Glaze (Optional):
- In a small bowl, whisk together the powdered sugar and fresh lemon juice until smooth and pourable.
- Drizzle the glaze over the cooled muffins.

Serve and Enjoy:
- Enjoy these lemon poppy seed muffins warm or at room temperature. They are perfect for breakfast, brunch, or as a snack with tea or coffee.

Notes:

- If you prefer a less sweet muffin, you can reduce the amount of sugar in the batter.
- Make sure to zest the lemons before juicing them for maximum flavor.
- Store leftover muffins in an airtight container at room temperature for 2-3 days, or freeze them for longer storage. Heat briefly in the microwave or oven before serving if desired.

**Cherry Bakewell Tartlets**

Ingredients:

*For the Pastry:*

- 1 1/4 cups all-purpose flour
- 1/2 cup unsalted butter, cold and diced
- 1/4 cup granulated sugar
- 1 egg yolk
- 1-2 tablespoons cold water

*For the Almond Filling:*

- 1/2 cup unsalted butter, softened
- 1/2 cup granulated sugar
- 1 cup almond flour (ground almonds)
- 1 large egg
- 1/2 teaspoon almond extract

*For Assembly:*

- 1/4 cup cherry jam or preserves
- Maraschino cherries, halved (for decoration)
- Icing sugar, for dusting

Instructions:

Make the Pastry:
- In a food processor, pulse together the flour and cold diced butter until the mixture resembles breadcrumbs.
- Add the sugar, egg yolk, and 1-2 tablespoons of cold water. Pulse again until the dough starts to come together.
- Turn out the dough onto a lightly floured surface, knead briefly until smooth, then shape into a disc. Wrap in plastic wrap and refrigerate for at least 30 minutes.

Prepare the Almond Filling:
- In a mixing bowl, cream together the softened butter and granulated sugar until pale and fluffy.

- Add the almond flour, egg, and almond extract. Mix until well combined and smooth. Set aside.

Preheat the Oven:
- Preheat your oven to 350°F (175°C). Grease a mini tart pan or line with mini tartlet cases.

Roll Out the Pastry:
- On a lightly floured surface, roll out the chilled pastry dough to about 1/8-inch thickness.
- Cut out rounds of dough slightly larger than the tartlet molds and press into the molds, trimming any excess dough.

Assemble the Tartlets:
- Spread about 1 teaspoon of cherry jam or preserves into the base of each pastry shell.
- Fill each tartlet with almond filling, smoothing the top with a spoon or spatula.

Bake the Tartlets:
- Place the filled tartlets on a baking sheet and bake in the preheated oven for 15-20 minutes, or until the pastry is golden and the almond filling is set.

Decorate and Serve:
- Remove the tartlets from the oven and let them cool in the pan for a few minutes.
- Gently press half a maraschino cherry into the center of each tartlet.
- Allow the tartlets to cool completely before dusting with icing sugar.

Serve and Enjoy:
- Serve these delightful cherry Bakewell tartlets as a sweet treat for afternoon tea or dessert. Enjoy!

Notes:

- You can use homemade or store-bought shortcrust pastry if preferred.
- If almond flour is not available, you can make your own by grinding blanched almonds in a food processor until finely ground.
- These tartlets can be stored in an airtight container at room temperature for 2-3 days. Enjoy them fresh or slightly warmed!

**Matcha Swirl Pound Cake**

Ingredients:

- 1 ½ cups all-purpose flour
- 1 teaspoon baking powder
- ¼ teaspoon salt
- 1 tablespoon matcha green tea powder
- 1 cup unsalted butter, softened
- 1 cup granulated sugar
- 4 large eggs
- 1 teaspoon vanilla extract
- ¼ cup milk

For the Matcha Swirl:

- 2 tablespoons matcha green tea powder
- 2 tablespoons hot water
- 2 tablespoons granulated sugar

Instructions:

1. Preheat Oven and Prepare Pan:
    - Preheat your oven to 350°F (175°C). Grease and flour a 9x5-inch loaf pan.
2. Mix Dry Ingredients:
    - In a medium bowl, whisk together the flour, baking powder, salt, and matcha powder. Set aside.
3. Make Matcha Swirl:
    - In a small bowl, mix the matcha powder and hot water until smooth. Stir in the sugar and set aside.
4. Prepare Batter:
    - In a large mixing bowl, beat the softened butter and sugar together until light and fluffy.
    - Add eggs, one at a time, beating well after each addition. Mix in the vanilla extract.
    - Gradually add the dry flour mixture into the wet ingredients, alternating with the milk. Begin and end with the flour mixture, mixing until just combined.
5. Swirl Batter with Matcha:
    - Pour half of the batter into the prepared loaf pan.
    - Dollop spoonfuls of the matcha mixture over the batter. Use a skewer or knife to gently swirl the matcha mixture into the batter.
    - Pour the remaining batter over the matcha swirl layer.
6. Bake:
    - Bake in the preheated oven for 50-60 minutes, or until a toothpick inserted into the center comes out clean.
7. Cool and Serve:

- Allow the cake to cool in the pan for about 15 minutes, then transfer to a wire rack to cool completely.
- Slice and serve the Matcha Swirl Pound Cake. Enjoy!

This Matcha Swirl Pound Cake is perfect for tea time or as a delightful dessert. The earthy matcha flavor combined with the richness of a pound cake makes for a unique and delicious treat.

**Coconut Macaroons**

Ingredients:

- 3 cups sweetened shredded coconut
- 3/4 cup sweetened condensed milk
- 2 teaspoons vanilla extract
- 2 large egg whites
- 1/4 teaspoon salt

Optional Toppings:

- Melted chocolate for dipping (dark, milk, or white chocolate)
- Chopped nuts (like almonds or pecans)

Instructions:

1. Preheat Oven and Prepare Baking Sheet:
    - Preheat your oven to 325°F (160°C). Line a baking sheet with parchment paper or silicone baking mat.
2. Mix Ingredients:
    - In a large bowl, combine the shredded coconut, sweetened condensed milk, and vanilla extract. Mix until well combined.
3. Whip Egg Whites:
    - In a separate bowl, beat the egg whites and salt using a hand mixer or stand mixer until stiff peaks form.
4. Combine Mixtures:
    - Gently fold the whipped egg whites into the coconut mixture until everything is evenly combined.
5. Form Macaroons:
    - Scoop about 2 tablespoons of the mixture and form into mounds using your hands or a cookie scoop. Place the mounds onto the prepared baking sheet, spacing them about 1 inch apart.
6. Bake:
    - Bake the macaroons in the preheated oven for 20-25 minutes or until the edges are golden brown.
7. Cool and Decorate:
    - Allow the macaroons to cool on the baking sheet for a few minutes, then transfer them to a wire rack to cool completely.
8. Optional Toppings:

- If desired, you can dip the cooled macaroons in melted chocolate. Simply melt your preferred chocolate (dark, milk, or white) in the microwave or using a double boiler. Dip the bottom of each macaroon into the melted chocolate and place back on the parchment paper to set.
- You can also sprinkle chopped nuts over the melted chocolate before it sets for added flavor and texture.

9. Serve and Enjoy:
    - Once the chocolate has set, your coconut macaroons are ready to be enjoyed! Store any leftover macaroons in an airtight container at room temperature for several days.

These coconut macaroons are wonderfully chewy on the inside and crispy on the outside, with a delicious coconut flavor that's hard to resist. They make a perfect treat for parties, gatherings, or simply as a sweet snack. Enjoy!

**Mini Pizzas**

Ingredients:

- English muffins or small pizza crusts (pre-made or homemade)
- Pizza sauce (store-bought or homemade)
- Shredded mozzarella cheese
- Toppings of your choice (pepperoni, sliced bell peppers, onions, mushrooms, olives, cooked sausage, etc.)
- Olive oil (optional)
- Italian seasoning or dried oregano (optional)
- Salt and pepper (to taste)

Instructions:

1. Preheat Oven:
    - Preheat your oven to 400°F (200°C) and line a baking sheet with parchment paper or foil.
2. Prepare English Muffins or Pizza Crusts:
    - If using English muffins, split them in half. If using small pizza crusts, leave them whole.
3. Assemble Mini Pizzas:
    - Place the English muffin halves or pizza crusts on the prepared baking sheet.
    - Spread a tablespoon or two of pizza sauce onto each muffin half or crust, leaving a small border around the edges.
4. Add Cheese and Toppings:
    - Sprinkle shredded mozzarella cheese evenly over the sauce.
    - Add your desired toppings. Be creative and mix different toppings for variety.
5. Optional Seasoning:
    - If desired, drizzle a little olive oil over the pizzas for added flavor and a golden finish.
    - Sprinkle Italian seasoning or dried oregano, along with a pinch of salt and pepper, over the top.
6. Bake:
    - Place the assembled mini pizzas in the preheated oven and bake for about 10-12 minutes, or until the cheese is melted and bubbly, and the edges of the crusts are golden brown.
7. Cool and Serve:
    - Remove the mini pizzas from the oven and let them cool slightly on the baking sheet.
    - Use a spatula to transfer them to a serving plate or board.
    - Slice the pizzas into halves or quarters if desired, and serve warm.

These mini pizzas are perfect for parties, after-school snacks, or a quick dinner option. Feel free to customize the toppings based on your preferences or what you have on hand. Kids and adults alike will enjoy these delicious and easy-to-make mini pizzas!

**Rosewater Shortbread**

Ingredients:

- 1 cup (2 sticks) unsalted butter, softened
- 1/2 cup granulated sugar
- 1 tablespoon rosewater
- 2 cups all-purpose flour
- 1/4 teaspoon salt
- Pink food coloring (optional)
- Edible rose petals or chopped pistachios for garnish (optional)

Instructions:

1. Preheat Oven:
    - Preheat your oven to 350°F (175°C) and line a baking sheet with parchment paper.
2. Cream Butter and Sugar:
    - In a mixing bowl, cream together the softened butter and granulated sugar until light and fluffy.
3. Add Rosewater and Flour:
    - Mix in the rosewater until well combined.
    - Gradually add the flour and salt to the butter mixture, mixing until a dough forms. If desired, add a drop or two of pink food coloring to tint the dough.
4. Shape the Dough:
    - Transfer the dough onto a lightly floured surface and gently knead it a few times until smooth.
    - Roll out the dough to about 1/4-inch thickness using a rolling pin.
5. Cut Out Cookies:
    - Use cookie cutters of your choice to cut out shapes from the dough. Alternatively, you can use a knife to cut the dough into squares or rectangles.
6. Arrange on Baking Sheet:
    - Place the cut-out cookies on the prepared baking sheet, spacing them slightly apart.
7. Chill (Optional):
    - For best results, chill the cookies in the refrigerator for about 15-20 minutes before baking. This helps the cookies retain their shape.
8. Bake:

- Bake the cookies in the preheated oven for 10-12 minutes, or until the edges are lightly golden.

9. Cool and Decorate:
    - Allow the cookies to cool on the baking sheet for a few minutes, then transfer them to a wire rack to cool completely.
10. Garnish (Optional):
    - Once cooled, you can optionally garnish the cookies with edible rose petals or chopped pistachios for a beautiful presentation and extra flavor.
11. Serve and Enjoy:
    - Serve these delightful rosewater shortbread cookies with tea or coffee. They make a lovely treat for special occasions or as homemade gifts.

These rosewater shortbread cookies have a subtle floral fragrance and a buttery, melt-in-your-mouth texture that's simply irresistible. Enjoy the delicate flavors of rosewater in every bite!

**Mini Eclairs with Coffee Cream**

Ingredients:

For the Eclairs:

- 1/2 cup water
- 1/4 cup unsalted butter
- 1/2 cup all-purpose flour
- 2 large eggs
- Pinch of salt

For the Coffee Cream Filling:

- 1 cup heavy cream
- 2 tablespoons granulated sugar
- 1 teaspoon instant coffee granules (or more to taste)
- 1/2 teaspoon vanilla extract

For the Chocolate Glaze (optional):

- 1/2 cup semi-sweet chocolate chips
- 2 tablespoons heavy cream

Instructions:

For the Eclairs:

1. Preheat Oven and Prepare Baking Sheet:
    - Preheat your oven to 400°F (200°C) and line a baking sheet with parchment paper.
2. Make Choux Pastry:
    - In a saucepan, bring water and butter to a boil. Add flour and salt all at once, stirring vigorously until the mixture forms a ball and pulls away from the sides of the pan.
3. Cool and Add Eggs:
    - Remove from heat and let cool slightly. Beat in eggs, one at a time, beating well after each addition, until the dough is smooth and glossy.
4. Pipe and Bake:
    - Transfer the dough to a piping bag fitted with a large round tip. Pipe 3-inch lengths of dough onto the prepared baking sheet, leaving space between each for expansion.

- Bake in the preheated oven for 15-20 minutes or until golden brown and puffed. Reduce heat to 350°F (175°C) and bake for an additional 10 minutes to dry out the centers. Remove from oven and let cool completely.

For the Coffee Cream Filling:

1. Prepare Coffee Cream:
    - In a mixing bowl, combine heavy cream, sugar, instant coffee granules, and vanilla extract.
    - Whip the mixture using a hand mixer or stand mixer until stiff peaks form and the cream is thick and smooth. Adjust the amount of coffee granules to taste.

For Assembly:

1. Fill Eclairs:
    - Once the eclairs are completely cooled, use a sharp knife to make a small slit along the side of each eclair.
    - Transfer the coffee cream filling into a piping bag fitted with a small round tip. Gently pipe the cream into each eclair until filled.
2. Optional Chocolate Glaze:
    - In a microwave-safe bowl, combine chocolate chips and heavy cream. Microwave in 30-second intervals, stirring in between, until the chocolate is melted and smooth.
    - Dip the top of each filled eclair into the chocolate glaze, allowing any excess to drip off. Place on a wire rack to set.
3. Chill and Serve:
    - Chill the filled eclairs in the refrigerator for at least 30 minutes to set the cream and chocolate glaze.
    - Serve chilled and enjoy these delightful mini eclairs with coffee cream as a decadent dessert!

These mini eclairs with coffee cream are perfect for special occasions or afternoon tea. The combination of delicate pastry, creamy coffee filling, and optional chocolate glaze makes them irresistible!

**Gingerbread Cookies**

Ingredients:

For the Gingerbread Cookies:

- 3 cups all-purpose flour
- 1 teaspoon baking powder
- 1/2 teaspoon baking soda
- 1/4 teaspoon salt
- 1 tablespoon ground ginger
- 1 1/2 teaspoons ground cinnamon
- 1/2 teaspoon ground cloves
- 1/2 teaspoon ground nutmeg
- 1/2 cup unsalted butter, softened
- 1/2 cup packed brown sugar
- 1 large egg
- 1/2 cup molasses
- 1 teaspoon vanilla extract

For Decorating (optional):

- Royal icing
- Sprinkles
- Candies

Instructions:

1. Prepare Dough:
   - In a bowl, whisk together flour, baking powder, baking soda, salt, ginger, cinnamon, cloves, and nutmeg. Set aside.
   - In a separate large bowl, beat together softened butter and brown sugar until creamy and smooth.
   - Add the egg, molasses, and vanilla extract to the butter-sugar mixture, and beat until well combined.
2. Combine Wet and Dry Ingredients:
   - Gradually add the dry flour mixture to the wet ingredients, mixing until a dough forms. If the dough is too sticky, add a little more flour.
3. Chill the Dough:

- Divide the dough into two equal parts, form each into a disc, wrap in plastic wrap, and chill in the refrigerator for at least 1 hour (or up to overnight).

4. Preheat Oven:
   - Preheat your oven to 350°F (175°C) and line baking sheets with parchment paper.
5. Roll Out Dough:
   - On a lightly floured surface, roll out one disc of dough to about 1/4-inch thickness. Use cookie cutters to cut out shapes.
   - Place the cut-out cookies onto the prepared baking sheets, spacing them slightly apart.
6. Bake the Cookies:
   - Bake in the preheated oven for 8-10 minutes, or until the edges are firm. Remove from oven and let cool on the baking sheets for a few minutes, then transfer to wire racks to cool completely.
7. Decorate (Optional):
   - Once the cookies are completely cooled, decorate with royal icing, sprinkles, or candies. Let the icing set before serving or storing the cookies.
8. Enjoy:
   - Enjoy these delightful gingerbread cookies with a cup of hot cocoa or tea! They make wonderful gifts and festive treats for holiday gatherings.

Feel free to get creative with the decorations and shapes of your gingerbread cookies. This recipe yields flavorful and aromatic cookies that are perfect for bringing the holiday spirit to your kitchen!

**Fig and Goat Cheese Crostini**

Ingredients:

- Baguette or crusty bread, sliced into 1/2-inch thick rounds
- Olive oil, for brushing
- 8 ounces soft goat cheese
- Fresh figs, sliced (about 8-10 figs)
- Honey, for drizzling
- Fresh thyme leaves, for garnish
- Salt and black pepper, to taste

Instructions:

1. Preheat Oven:
    - Preheat your oven to 375°F (190°C).
2. Prepare Bread:
    - Arrange the bread slices on a baking sheet. Brush both sides of each slice with olive oil.
3. Toast Bread:
    - Bake the bread slices in the preheated oven for about 8-10 minutes, flipping halfway through, until they are golden and crisp. Remove from the oven and let them cool slightly.
4. Assemble Crostini:
    - Spread a generous amount of goat cheese on each toasted bread slice.
5. Add Sliced Figs:
    - Place 1-2 slices of fresh figs on top of the goat cheese layer on each crostini.
6. Drizzle with Honey:
    - Drizzle honey over the figs and goat cheese. The sweetness of honey complements the flavors perfectly.
7. Season and Garnish:
    - Sprinkle a pinch of salt and freshly ground black pepper over the crostini.
    - Garnish with fresh thyme leaves for added flavor and presentation.
8. Serve:
    - Arrange the fig and goat cheese crostini on a serving platter or board.
    - Serve immediately and enjoy as a delicious appetizer or snack.

These fig and goat cheese crostini are perfect for entertaining guests or as a special treat for yourself. They offer a delightful combination of textures and flavors that will surely impress! Adjust the quantities based on your preferences and the number of guests you're serving.

**Linzer Cookies**

Ingredients:

For the Cookie Dough:

- 1 cup (2 sticks) unsalted butter, softened
- 3/4 cup granulated sugar
- 1 large egg
- 1 teaspoon vanilla extract
- 2 cups all-purpose flour
- 1 cup finely ground almonds (almond meal)
- 1/2 teaspoon ground cinnamon
- 1/4 teaspoon salt
- Confectioners' sugar, for dusting

For Filling and Assembly:

- Raspberry jam or any preferred jam or preserves
- Confectioners' sugar, for dusting

Instructions:

1. Prepare Cookie Dough:
    - In a large mixing bowl, cream together the softened butter and granulated sugar until light and fluffy.
    - Add the egg and vanilla extract, and beat until well combined.
2. Mix Dry Ingredients:
    - In a separate bowl, whisk together the flour, ground almonds, cinnamon, and salt.
3. Combine Wet and Dry Ingredients:
    - Gradually add the dry ingredient mixture to the butter mixture, mixing until a dough forms.
    - Divide the dough into two equal portions, flatten into discs, wrap in plastic wrap, and refrigerate for at least 1 hour (or up to overnight) until firm.
4. Preheat Oven:
    - Preheat your oven to 350°F (175°C) and line baking sheets with parchment paper.
5. Roll Out Dough:
    - On a lightly floured surface, roll out one disc of chilled dough to about 1/8-inch thickness.
    - Use a round cookie cutter to cut out cookies. For half of the cookies, use a smaller round cutter to cut out the centers, creating a "window" effect.
6. Bake Cookies:

- Place the cookies on the prepared baking sheets and bake for 10-12 minutes, or until the edges are lightly golden.
- Remove from the oven and let the cookies cool on the baking sheets for a few minutes before transferring to wire racks to cool completely.

7. Assemble Linzer Cookies:
    - Spread a thin layer of raspberry jam (or your preferred jam) on the bottom (solid) cookies.
    - Dust the top (window) cookies with confectioners' sugar.
    - Place the sugared top cookies gently on top of the jam-covered bottom cookies to create sandwich cookies.
8. Serve and Enjoy:
    - Arrange the Linzer cookies on a serving platter and dust with additional confectioners' sugar if desired.
    - These cookies are best enjoyed with a cup of tea or coffee.

Linzer cookies are not only delicious but also beautiful with their intricate designs. They make lovely gifts and are perfect for festive occasions. Experiment with different types of jams or preserves to create unique flavor combinations!

**Sausage Rolls**

Ingredients:

For the Sausage Filling:

- 1 lb (450g) ground pork or sausage meat
- 1 small onion, finely chopped
- 2 cloves garlic, minced
- 1 teaspoon dried sage
- 1/2 teaspoon dried thyme
- Salt and pepper, to taste
- 1 tablespoon Worcestershire sauce (optional)

For the Pastry:

- 2 sheets of puff pastry, thawed if frozen
- 1 large egg, beaten (for egg wash)

Instructions:

1. Preheat Oven:
    - Preheat your oven to 400°F (200°C) and line a baking sheet with parchment paper.
2. Prepare Sausage Filling:
    - In a mixing bowl, combine the ground pork (or sausage meat), finely chopped onion, minced garlic, dried sage, dried thyme, salt, pepper, and Worcestershire sauce (if using). Mix well until all ingredients are evenly incorporated.
3. Assemble Sausage Rolls:
    - Lay out one sheet of puff pastry on a lightly floured surface. Cut the pastry sheet in half lengthwise to make two long rectangles.
    - Divide the sausage filling into two portions. Shape each portion into a long, thin log along the length of each pastry rectangle.
    - Brush one edge of the pastry with beaten egg. Roll the pastry over the sausage filling, sealing the edges by pressing gently with your fingers. Repeat with the second pastry sheet and remaining sausage filling.
4. Cut and Score:
    - Using a sharp knife, cut each long roll into smaller sausage rolls, about 2-inch lengths. Score the top of each roll with a sharp knife to create a decorative pattern.
5. Brush with Egg Wash:
    - Place the sausage rolls on the prepared baking sheet. Brush the tops of the rolls with the remaining beaten egg for a golden finish.
6. Bake:

- Bake in the preheated oven for 20-25 minutes, or until the pastry is golden brown and cooked through.

7. Serve:
    - Remove the sausage rolls from the oven and let them cool slightly on a wire rack.
    - Serve the sausage rolls warm as a snack or appetizer. They are delicious on their own or with your favorite dipping sauce (such as ketchup or mustard).

These homemade sausage rolls are perfect for parties, picnics, or anytime you crave a tasty savory treat. You can also customize the filling with different herbs or spices to suit your taste. Enjoy these golden, flaky delights!

**Apple Turnovers**

Ingredients:

For the Apple Filling:

- 2 large apples (such as Granny Smith or Honeycrisp), peeled, cored, and diced
- 2 tablespoons unsalted butter
- 1/4 cup granulated sugar
- 1 teaspoon ground cinnamon
- 1/4 teaspoon ground nutmeg
- 1 tablespoon lemon juice
- 1 tablespoon all-purpose flour

For Assembly:

- 1 package (2 sheets) of frozen puff pastry, thawed
- 1 large egg, beaten (for egg wash)
- Granulated sugar, for sprinkling

Instructions:

1. Prepare the Apple Filling:
    - In a saucepan, melt the butter over medium heat. Add the diced apples, granulated sugar, cinnamon, nutmeg, and lemon juice.
    - Cook, stirring occasionally, until the apples are tender and the mixture is syrupy, about 8-10 minutes.
    - Stir in the flour to thicken the filling. Remove from heat and let it cool slightly.
2. Preheat Oven:
    - Preheat your oven to 375°F (190°C) and line a baking sheet with parchment paper.
3. Roll Out Puff Pastry:
    - On a lightly floured surface, unfold one sheet of puff pastry. Roll it out slightly to smooth any creases and to make it slightly thinner.
    - Cut the pastry into 4 squares.
4. Fill and Seal Turnovers:
    - Place a spoonful of the cooled apple filling in the center of each pastry square.
    - Brush the edges of the pastry with beaten egg.

- Fold each pastry square diagonally to form a triangle, enclosing the apple filling. Press the edges with a fork to seal.
5. Repeat with Remaining Ingredients:
    - Repeat the process with the second sheet of puff pastry and remaining apple filling.
6. Brush with Egg Wash and Sprinkle with Sugar:
    - Place the turnovers on the prepared baking sheet. Brush the tops with the remaining beaten egg and sprinkle with granulated sugar for a golden finish.
7. Bake:
    - Bake in the preheated oven for 20-25 minutes, or until the turnovers are puffed and golden brown.
8. Cool and Serve:
    - Remove the apple turnovers from the oven and let them cool slightly on a wire rack.
    - Serve warm or at room temperature. Enjoy these delicious apple turnovers on their own or with a scoop of vanilla ice cream.

These homemade apple turnovers are perfect for breakfast, brunch, or dessert. They are best enjoyed fresh from the oven when the pastry is crisp and flaky. Feel free to customize the filling with additional spices or add-ins like raisins or chopped nuts. Enjoy!

**Chocolate Hazelnut Biscotti**

Ingredients:

- 1 3/4 cups all-purpose flour
- 1/2 cup unsweetened cocoa powder
- 1 teaspoon baking powder
- 1/4 teaspoon salt
- 1/2 cup unsalted butter, softened
- 3/4 cup granulated sugar
- 2 large eggs
- 1 teaspoon vanilla extract
- 1 cup hazelnuts, toasted, skins removed, and coarsely chopped
- 1/2 cup semisweet or dark chocolate chips or chunks

Instructions:

1. Preheat Oven:
    - Preheat your oven to 350°F (175°C). Line a baking sheet with parchment paper.
2. Toast and Skin Hazelnuts:
    - Spread the hazelnuts on a baking sheet and toast in the preheated oven for about 10-12 minutes, or until fragrant and the skins start to crack.
    - Remove from the oven and let cool slightly. Rub the hazelnuts with a kitchen towel to remove the skins. Coarsely chop the hazelnuts and set aside.
3. Prepare Dry Ingredients:
    - In a bowl, whisk together the flour, cocoa powder, baking powder, and salt. Set aside.
4. Cream Butter and Sugar:
    - In a separate bowl, cream together the softened butter and granulated sugar until light and fluffy.
5. Add Eggs and Vanilla:
    - Beat in the eggs, one at a time, until well combined. Mix in the vanilla extract.
6. Combine Wet and Dry Ingredients:
    - Gradually add the dry flour mixture to the wet ingredients, mixing until a dough forms.
7. Add Hazelnuts and Chocolate:
    - Fold in the chopped hazelnuts and chocolate chips/chunks into the dough until evenly distributed.
8. Shape Dough:
    - Divide the dough in half. On a lightly floured surface, shape each half into a log about 12 inches long and 2 inches wide. Place the logs on the prepared baking sheet, spacing them apart.
9. Bake First Time:
    - Bake in the preheated oven for 25-30 minutes, or until firm to the touch. Remove from the oven and let cool on the baking sheet for 10 minutes.

10. Slice Biscotti:
    - Using a sharp knife, slice the logs diagonally into 1/2-inch thick slices. Arrange the biscotti cut-side down on the baking sheet.
11. Bake Second Time:
    - Return the biscotti to the oven and bake for an additional 10-12 minutes, or until the biscotti are crisp and dry. Remove from the oven and let cool completely on wire racks.
12. Enjoy:
    - Once cooled, these chocolate hazelnut biscotti are ready to be enjoyed! Store in an airtight container at room temperature for up to two weeks.

These chocolate hazelnut biscotti are perfect for gifting during the holidays or enjoying with a cup of coffee or tea. The combination of rich cocoa, crunchy hazelnuts, and chocolate chunks makes these biscotti irresistible!

**Plum Cake**

Ingredients:

- 1 1/2 cups all-purpose flour
- 1 1/2 teaspoons baking powder
- 1/4 teaspoon salt
- 1/2 cup unsalted butter, softened
- 3/4 cup granulated sugar
- 2 large eggs
- 1 teaspoon vanilla extract
- 1/3 cup sour cream or Greek yogurt
- 4-5 plums, pitted and sliced
- 2 tablespoons brown sugar
- 1/2 teaspoon ground cinnamon
- Powdered sugar, for dusting (optional)

Instructions:

1. Preheat Oven and Prepare Pan:
    - Preheat your oven to 350°F (175°C). Grease a 9-inch round cake pan and line the bottom with parchment paper.
2. Prepare Dry Ingredients:
    - In a bowl, whisk together the flour, baking powder, and salt. Set aside.
3. Cream Butter and Sugar:
    - In a separate large mixing bowl, cream together the softened butter and granulated sugar until light and fluffy.
4. Add Eggs and Vanilla:
    - Beat in the eggs, one at a time, until well combined. Mix in the vanilla extract.
5. Combine Wet and Dry Ingredients:
    - Gradually add the dry flour mixture to the wet ingredients, alternating with the sour cream (or Greek yogurt), beginning and ending with the flour mixture. Mix until just combined.
6. Prepare Plum Topping:
    - In a small bowl, combine the sliced plums, brown sugar, and ground cinnamon. Toss gently to coat the plums.
7. Assemble Cake:
    - Spread the cake batter evenly into the prepared cake pan.
    - Arrange the plum slices on top of the batter in a decorative pattern.

8. Bake:
    - Bake in the preheated oven for 40-45 minutes, or until the cake is golden brown and a toothpick inserted into the center comes out clean.
9. Cool and Serve:
    - Allow the cake to cool in the pan for about 10 minutes before transferring to a wire rack to cool completely.
    - Dust with powdered sugar before serving, if desired.
10. Enjoy:
    - Slice and serve this delightful plum cake as a delicious dessert or afternoon treat. It's perfect served warm with a dollop of whipped cream or vanilla ice cream.

This plum cake is a wonderful way to enjoy fresh plums when they are in season. The combination of moist cake and juicy, sweet-tart plums is simply irresistible!

**Mini Lemon Tarts**

Ingredients:

For the Tart Shells:

- 1 1/4 cups all-purpose flour
- 1/2 cup unsalted butter, cold and cubed
- 1/4 cup granulated sugar
- 1 large egg yolk
- 1-2 tablespoons ice water

For the Lemon Filling:

- 3/4 cup granulated sugar
- 3 large eggs
- 1/2 cup fresh lemon juice (from about 3-4 lemons)
- Zest of 1 lemon
- 1/4 cup unsalted butter, melted
- Powdered sugar, for dusting (optional)

Instructions:

For the Tart Shells:

1. Prepare Tart Dough:
    - In a food processor, pulse together the flour and sugar until combined.
    - Add the cold, cubed butter and pulse until the mixture resembles coarse crumbs.
    - Add the egg yolk and 1 tablespoon of ice water. Pulse until the dough starts to come together. If needed, add an additional tablespoon of ice water.
2. Form Dough:
    - Turn the dough out onto a clean surface and gently knead it a few times until it forms a smooth ball.
    - Flatten the dough into a disc, wrap it in plastic wrap, and refrigerate for at least 30 minutes.
3. Preheat Oven and Prepare Tart Shells:
    - Preheat your oven to 375°F (190°C). Lightly grease a mini muffin tin.
    - Roll out the chilled dough on a floured surface to about 1/8-inch thickness.

- Use a round cookie cutter slightly larger than the mini muffin tin cavities to cut out circles of dough.
- Gently press each circle of dough into the mini muffin tin cavities, shaping them into mini tart shells.

4. Bake Tart Shells:
   - Prick the bottoms of the tart shells with a fork to prevent puffing.
   - Bake in the preheated oven for 10-12 minutes, or until the tart shells are golden brown. Remove from the oven and let cool completely.

For the Lemon Filling:

1. Prepare Lemon Filling:
   - In a bowl, whisk together the granulated sugar and eggs until well combined.
   - Whisk in the fresh lemon juice and lemon zest until smooth.
   - Gradually whisk in the melted butter until the mixture is well combined.
2. Fill Tart Shells:
   - Spoon the lemon filling into the cooled tart shells, filling each one almost to the top.
3. Bake Lemon Tarts:
   - Bake the filled tart shells in the preheated oven for 12-15 minutes, or until the lemon filling is set.
   - Remove from the oven and let the tarts cool in the mini muffin tin for a few minutes before transferring to a wire rack to cool completely.
4. Serve:
   - Once cooled, dust the mini lemon tarts with powdered sugar if desired.
   - Serve these delicious mini lemon tarts as a delightful dessert or sweet snack.

Enjoy these mini lemon tarts with their tangy, refreshing lemon filling and buttery tart shells. They are sure to be a hit at any gathering!

**Nutella Swirl Brownies**

Ingredients:

- 1/2 cup (1 stick) unsalted butter
- 1 cup granulated sugar
- 2 large eggs
- 1 teaspoon vanilla extract
- 1/3 cup unsweetened cocoa powder
- 1/2 cup all-purpose flour
- 1/4 teaspoon salt
- 1/2 cup Nutella (or other chocolate hazelnut spread)

Instructions:

1. Preheat Oven and Prepare Pan:
    - Preheat your oven to 350°F (175°C). Grease an 8x8-inch baking pan or line it with parchment paper.
2. Melt Butter:
    - In a microwave-safe bowl, melt the butter in the microwave in short intervals until completely melted.
3. Mix Wet Ingredients:
    - In a separate bowl, whisk together the melted butter and granulated sugar until well combined.
    - Add the eggs and vanilla extract to the butter-sugar mixture, and whisk until smooth.
4. Add Dry Ingredients:
    - Sift in the cocoa powder, all-purpose flour, and salt into the wet ingredients.
    - Gently fold the dry ingredients into the wet ingredients until just combined. Be careful not to overmix.
5. Prepare Nutella Swirl:
    - Microwave the Nutella in a microwave-safe bowl for a few seconds to soften it slightly.
    - Pour half of the brownie batter into the prepared baking pan. Drop spoonfuls of Nutella over the batter.
    - Use a knife or skewer to swirl the Nutella into the batter to create a marbled effect.
    - Pour the remaining brownie batter over the Nutella swirl layer.
6. Create Swirl Pattern:
    - Add more spoonfuls of Nutella over the top layer of brownie batter.
    - Use a knife or skewer to swirl the Nutella into the top layer of batter to create a decorative swirl pattern.
7. Bake:
    - Bake in the preheated oven for 20-25 minutes, or until a toothpick inserted into the center comes out with a few moist crumbs (not wet batter).

8. Cool and Serve:
    - Allow the Nutella swirl brownies to cool completely in the pan on a wire rack.
    - Once cooled, lift the brownies out of the pan using the parchment paper (if using), and cut into squares.
    - Serve and enjoy these indulgent Nutella swirl brownies with a glass of milk or a scoop of vanilla ice cream.

These Nutella swirl brownies are perfect for satisfying your chocolate cravings. The Nutella adds a delightful hazelnut flavor and a beautiful swirl pattern to these rich and fudgy brownies. They are sure to be a hit with Nutella lovers of all ages!

**Raspberry Ripple Cheesecake Bars**

Ingredients:

For the Crust:

- 1 1/2 cups graham cracker crumbs (about 10-12 graham crackers)
- 1/4 cup granulated sugar
- 1/2 cup unsalted butter, melted

For the Cheesecake Filling:

- 16 oz (2 packages) cream cheese, softened
- 1/2 cup granulated sugar
- 2 large eggs
- 1 teaspoon vanilla extract
- 1/2 cup sour cream

For the Raspberry Swirl:

- 1 cup fresh or frozen raspberries
- 2 tablespoons granulated sugar
- 1 tablespoon water
- 1 tablespoon cornstarch

Instructions:

1. Preheat Oven and Prepare Pan:
    - Preheat your oven to 325°F (160°C). Line an 8x8-inch baking pan with parchment paper, leaving an overhang for easy removal.
2. Make the Crust:
    - In a bowl, mix together the graham cracker crumbs, granulated sugar, and melted butter until combined.
    - Press the mixture evenly into the bottom of the prepared baking pan.
3. Bake the Crust:
    - Bake the crust in the preheated oven for 10 minutes. Remove from the oven and let it cool slightly while you prepare the filling.
4. Make the Raspberry Swirl:
    - In a small saucepan, combine the raspberries, granulated sugar, water, and cornstarch.
    - Cook over medium heat, stirring constantly, until the mixture comes to a boil and thickens slightly (about 3-4 minutes).

- Remove from heat and strain through a fine mesh sieve to remove the seeds. Set aside to cool.
5. Make the Cheesecake Filling:
    - In a large mixing bowl, beat the softened cream cheese and granulated sugar until smooth and creamy.
    - Add the eggs, one at a time, beating well after each addition.
    - Mix in the vanilla extract and sour cream until smooth and combined.
6. Assemble and Swirl:
    - Pour the cheesecake filling over the cooled crust.
    - Drop spoonfuls of the raspberry sauce over the top of the cheesecake filling.
    - Use a toothpick or knife to gently swirl the raspberry sauce into the cheesecake filling, creating a marbled effect.
7. Bake the Cheesecake Bars:
    - Bake in the preheated oven for 35-40 minutes, or until the edges are set and the center is slightly jiggly.
    - Remove from the oven and let the cheesecake bars cool completely in the pan on a wire rack.
8. Chill and Serve:
    - Once cooled, refrigerate the cheesecake bars for at least 3-4 hours or overnight until firm.
    - Lift the cheesecake bars out of the pan using the parchment paper overhang, and cut into squares.
    - Serve chilled and enjoy these raspberry ripple cheesecake bars as a delightful dessert!

These raspberry ripple cheesecake bars are creamy, tangy, and bursting with raspberry flavor. They make a perfect dessert for parties, gatherings, or simply as a sweet treat to enjoy any time.

**Green Tea Ice Cream**

Ingredients:

- 2 cups heavy cream
- 1 cup whole milk
- 2/3 cup granulated sugar
- 3 tablespoons matcha green tea powder
- 4 large egg yolks
- 1 teaspoon vanilla extract

Instructions:

1. Prepare Ice Cream Base:
    - In a saucepan, combine the heavy cream, whole milk, and granulated sugar over medium heat. Whisk until the sugar is dissolved and the mixture is heated through (do not boil).
2. Whisk in Matcha Powder:
    - Remove the saucepan from heat. Whisk in the matcha green tea powder until completely dissolved and the mixture is smooth. Set aside.
3. Temper the Egg Yolks:
    - In a separate bowl, whisk the egg yolks until smooth.
    - Gradually add a ladleful of the warm matcha cream mixture into the egg yolks, whisking constantly. This process will temper the egg yolks to prevent them from curdling when added to the hot mixture.
4. Combine and Cook the Custard:
    - Pour the tempered egg yolk mixture back into the saucepan with the remaining matcha cream mixture, whisking constantly.
    - Cook the mixture over medium-low heat, stirring constantly with a wooden spoon or spatula, until it thickens slightly and coats the back of the spoon (about 5-7 minutes). Do not let it boil.
5. Strain and Chill:
    - Remove the custard from heat and strain it through a fine-mesh sieve into a clean bowl to remove any lumps.
    - Stir in the vanilla extract. Cover the bowl with plastic wrap, placing the wrap directly on the surface of the custard to prevent a skin from forming.
    - Refrigerate the custard until completely chilled, at least 4 hours or overnight.
6. Churn the Ice Cream:
    - Once chilled, pour the matcha custard into an ice cream maker and churn according to the manufacturer's instructions until the mixture reaches a soft-serve consistency.
7. Freeze the Ice Cream:
    - Transfer the churned ice cream into an airtight container. Smooth the top with a spatula, then cover with plastic wrap or parchment paper directly on the surface of the ice cream to prevent ice crystals from forming.

- Freeze the green tea ice cream for at least 4 hours or until firm.
8. Serve and Enjoy:
    - Scoop the green tea ice cream into bowls or cones, and enjoy this delightful homemade treat!

This homemade green tea ice cream is creamy, smooth, and bursting with matcha flavor. It's a perfect dessert for green tea lovers and a refreshing way to cool down on a hot day. Garnish with additional matcha powder or whipped cream if desired. Enjoy!

www.ingramcontent.com/pod-product-compliance
Lightning Source LLC
LaVergne TN
LVHW081605060526
838201LV00054B/2085